Elegant Objects

by Yegor Bugayenko

Volume 1

Copyright © 2015-2020 by Yegor Bugayenko

All rights reserved. No part of the contents of this book may be reproduced or transmitted in any form or by any means without the written permission of the publisher.

Printed and bound in the United States of America.

Version: 1.7
Git hash: e7fdaf3
Date: September 9, 2020
Words: 14832
Vocabulary: 2284

ISBN: 978-1519166913
Place: Palo Alto, California, USA
Size: 223 pages
Recommended price: $40,96
Web: http://www.yegor256.com/elegant-objects.html

✉ book@yegor256.com 🐦 in 🐙 📷 f yegor256

Published by CreateSpace, an Amazon company.

"Step one in the transformation of a successful procedural developer into a successful object developer is a lobotomy"

–David West[1]

---

[1] David West, *Object Thinking*, Microsoft Press, 2004.

Contents

Acknowledgements		**9**
Preface		**11**
1	**Birth**	**17**
1.1	Never use -er names	19
1.2	Make one constructor primary	27
1.3	Keep constructors code-free	33
2	**Education**	**41**
2.1	Encapsulate as little as possible	42
2.2	Encapsulate something at the very least	46
2.3	Always use interfaces	50
2.4	Choose method names carefully	53
	2.4.1 Builders are nouns	55
	2.4.2 Manipulators are verbs	58
	2.4.3 Examples of both	60
	2.4.4 Boolean results	61
2.5	Don't use public constants	64
	2.5.1 Introduction of coupling	66
	2.5.2 Loss of cohesion	68
2.6	Be immutable	74
	2.6.1 Identity mutability	79
	2.6.2 Failure atomicity	80

5

		2.6.3	Temporal coupling 83
		2.6.4	Side effect-free 85
		2.6.5	No NULL references 86
		2.6.6	Thread safety 88
		2.6.7	Smaller and simpler objects 92
	2.7	Write tests instead of documentation 94
	2.8	Don't mock; use fakes 98
	2.9	Keep interfaces short; use smarts 107

3 Employment   113
    3.1 Expose fewer than five public methods 115
    3.2 Don't use static methods 117
          3.2.1 Object vs. computer thinking 119
          3.2.2 Declarative vs. imperative style 122
          3.2.3 Utility classes 132
          3.2.4 Singleton Pattern 133
          3.2.5 Functional programming 138
          3.2.6 Composable decorators 140
    3.3 Never accept NULL arguments 144
    3.4 Be loyal and immutable, or constant 151
    3.5 Never use getters and setters 162
          3.5.1 Objects vs. data structures 163
          3.5.2 Good intentions, bad outcome 166
          3.5.3 It's all about prefixes 168
    3.6 Don't use "new" outside of secondary ctors 171
    3.7 Avoid type introspection and casting 178

4 Retirement   183
    4.1 Never return NULL 185
          4.1.1 Fail fast vs. fail safe 189
          4.1.2 Alternatives to NULL 191
    4.2 Throw only checked exceptions 195

	4.2.1	Don't catch unless you have to 198
	4.2.2	Always chain exceptions 201
	4.2.3	Recover only once 203
	4.2.4	Use aspect-oriented programming 206
	4.2.5	Just one exception type is enough 208
4.3	Be either final or abstract 209
4.4	Use RAII 216

Epilogue   **219**

Index   **221**

Acknowledgements

Many thanks to these guys, who reviewed the book and helped me make it better and cleaner. The list is not in alphabetic order, but in order of importance of their contribution:

- Thanasis Papapanagiotou
- Francesco Bianchi
- Philip Buuck
- Kanstantsin Kamkou
- Andrei Istomin

This is a full list of contributors (in alphabetic order):
Alexey Abashev, Anton Arhipov, Francesco Bianchi, Ion Bordian,
Tamila Bugayenko, Philip Buuck, Fabrício Barros Cabral,
Anton Chernousov, Piotr Chmielowski, Nicole Cordes,
Igor Dmitriev, Aneesh Dogra, Viktor Gamov, Artem Gapchenko,
Quinn Gil, Konstantin Gukov, Andrei Istomin,
Kanstantsin Kamkou, Kiryl Karatsetski, Nicos Kekchidis,
Christian Köstlin, Janez Kuhar, Mateusz Oślislok, John Page,
Xiasong Pan, Thanasis Papapanagiotou, Alexey Patsev,
Efim Pyshnograev, Baruch Sadogursky,
Marcos Douglas B. Santos, Oksana Semenkova, Michal Švec,
Krzysztof Szafrański, Mauricio Togneri, Silas Reinagel,
Simon Tsai, Andrey Valyaev, Ilya Vassilevsky.

Want to see your name in this list in the next edition? Just send your thoughts to `book@yegor256.com`. I reply to all emails.

And, of course, thanks to Andreea Mironiuc for the cactus on the cover.

Preface

There have been many books written about Object-Oriented Programming (OOP). Why another? Because we are in trouble. We are getting further and further away from what OOP creators had in mind, and there is almost no hope of turning back. All existing OOP languages encourage us to treat objects as "data structures with attached procedures", which is a totally wrong and dangerous misconception. We create new languages, but they do the same or even worse. As object-oriented programmers, we are forced to think like procedural programmers thought 40 years ago. In other words, think like computers, not objects.

This book is a collection of practical recommendations that I believe can change the situation and stop the degradation of OOP. I learned most recommendations from the publications listed in the bibliography at the end of the book. Some of them I just made up.

There are 23 strands of advice, grouped into four chapters: birth, school, employment, and retirement. We'll talk about "Mr. Object," an anthropomorphized entity in the object-oriented world. He will be born, go to school, get hired to do some job for us, and then retire. We'll watch how it unfolds and try to learn something new. Together. Let's go.

Wait. You know, before publishing, I sent this book to a dozen reviewers and almost all of them complained about the absence of an intro. They said that I threw them blindly into the first theme, with no overall context. They also said that it was difficult to digest my ideas, having a lot of previous experience in Java/C++ programming. They found that what they think OOP is contradicts with my understanding of it. Long story short, they all demanded that I write an intro. So, here it is.

I believe that OOP was designed as a solution for the problems we had in *procedural* programming, especially in languages like C and COBOL. The procedural style of writing code is very easy to understand for those who understand how a CPU works, processing instructions one by one, and letting them manipulate the data in memory. A piece of code in C, also known as a "function," is a set of statements, which have to be executed in a chronological order, basically moving data from one place in memory to another and making some in-fly transformations with them. That's how it worked for years and it still works. There is a ton of software written in that style, including all major Unix operating systems, for example.

Technically, this approach works—the code compiles and runs. However, there are problems with *maintainability*. The author of the code can more or less easily understand how it works while he or she is writing it. However, when you look at that code later, it's rather difficult to figure out what the intention of its author was. In other words, it is written for computers, not for humans. The best example of such a procedural and imperative language is probably Assembly. It stays as close as possible to the CPU, is very far from the language we speak in real life. There is no such thing as customer, file, rectangle, or price in Assembly. There are only registers, bytes, bits, and pointers—the things a CPU understands very well.

That's how it was years ago, when computers were big, slow, and in charge. We had to learn and speak their language, not the other way around. This was mostly because we had to make our software fast in order to be useful. We were fighting for each processing instruction, for each byte of memory. We didn't really care much about maintainability, more about speed and memory usage. It is important to mention that twenty years ago, programmers were much cheaper than computers. Excuse me that comparison, but it's true. Hiring a new programmer was cheaper than buying a bigger hard disc. Sometimes it was not even possible to solve a performance problem with extra hardware. There was no faster or larger hardware! But programmers were rather cheap (you can try to find statistics about our salaries twenty years ago). That's why we had to do what CPUs told us to.

Fortunately, the situation started to change some time ago and the problem of maintainability became more important than speed and memory. The lifecycle of software products also started to grow and it became obvious that Assembly code simply can't survive a transfer from one team to another—the new team would always want to re-write from scratch instead of figuring out how that 5000-line listing works. I believe that's how higher-level programming paradigms started to appear, including functional, logical and object-oriented (there are more, but these three are the most popular, I think). They all were shifting the focus from computers to humans. They allowed us to speak our own language instead of the language our CPU was used to. They helped us make the code much easier to understand and therefore much more maintainable. That was the intention.

However, historically, OOP inherited a lot from procedural programming. Well, not OOP as a paradigm, but the languages that became popular and were declared object-oriented.

I'm talking mostly about C++ and Java. Others, like Ruby, simply followed the direction set by these big two. Maybe that was the reason why C++ became popular—because it looked very similar to C and was consequently easy to learn. Java was also designed to simplify the transition from C++—its syntax looked very much like C++ and was easy for C++ programmers to learn. Because of these two big compromised transitions (from C to C++ and from C++ to Java) we have OOP that looks very much like procedural C.

Even though we have classes and objects, we still have instructions, statements, and their chronological execution. We don't deal any more with pointers, memory manipulations, and CPU registers, but the core principle is still in place—we instruct our CPU what to do and we manipulate data in memory. You may say, what's wrong with that? Nothing is wrong, if you want to stay in the procedural domain. Just like nothing was wrong with Assembly. Except the fact that the code was not really maintainable. This is the same problem we have today with Java/Ruby/Python/etc software—it is not maintainable, because it never was object-oriented.

Our code has classes, methods, objects, inheritance, and polymorphism, but it's not really object-oriented. What exactly is wrong with it? This is what I'm trying to explain in this book. It's really difficult to say what I have to say in just a few paragraphs. You really have to read it all, in order to grasp the idea and the mindset of pure OOP.

I tried to make the material as practical as possible and illustrate ideas with realistic code examples. Moreover, almost every section here has a blog post on the same or a very relevant subject. You can find links to these blog posts at the beginnings of sections. Feel free to post your comments there and I'll try to reply and discuss. Honestly, I don't think I'm right in everything I'm saying here. I was a procedural programmer myself for many years. It's really difficult to forget it all and start thinking in objects, instead of instructions and statements. Thus, I will appreciate your feedback.

That was the intro. I don't think it gave you a lot of information, but at least you know now what we'll be talking about in the next two hundred pages. Be ready for a lot of controversy. And be brave to challenge yourself. Have fun!

Chapter 1

Birth

An object is a living organism—let's start from this. From the first page on, we'll do as much as we can to *anthropomorphize* it. We will be treating it as a human being, in other words. That's why I will use *he* to refer to an object. And my dear female readers, please don't be offended. I may sometimes be rude to a poor object and don't want to be rude to a woman. So in this book, an object is a male, a "he."

To start with, he lives inside his *scope of visibility*. For example, (I'm mainly using Java and will continue to do so; I hope you understand it):

```
if (price < 100) {
  Cash extra = new Cash(5);
  price.add(extra);
}
```

Object `extra` is visible only inside the `if` block—that is his scope of visibility. Why is that important now? Because an object is a living organism. We should define what his living environment is and will be before we breathe life into him. What remains within him and what lies outside? In this example, `price` is outside and the number `5` is inside, right?

By the way, before we continue, let me assure you that everything you are going to read in this book is very practical and pragmatic. Rather than waxing on about philosophy, the majority revolves around the practical application of object-oriented programming to real-life problems. The main goal I'm trying to achieve with this writing is to increase the *maintainability* of your code. Of our code.

Maintainability is an important quality of any kind of software, and it may be measured as the time required for me to understand your code. The longer it takes, the lower the maintainability and therefore the worse your code is. I would even say that *if I don't understand you, it's your fault*. By understanding objects and their roles in OOP, you will increase your code's maintainability. Your code will become shorter, easier to digest, more modular, more cohesive, etc. It will become better, which in most real-life projects means cheaper; that's it.

So please don't be surprised by my seemingly too philosophical and abstract discussions. They are indeed very practical.

Now, back to the scope of visibility. If I'm `extra`, then `price` is the world around me. Number `5` is inside me, and is my inner world. Well, this is not exactly right. For now, it is enough to agree that `price` is outside and `5` is inside. We'll get back to this again, though a bit later in Section 3.4.

1.1 Never use -er names

`Discuss at http://goo.gl/Uy3wZ6`

The first job, after you know the scope of visibility for a future object, is to invent a good name for its class.

But wait, let me step aside for a few minutes and discuss something else—the difference between an object and a class. I'm sure you understand what it is. A class is a *factory* of objects. Let me convince you, it's important.

A class makes objects, though we usually phrase that by saying a class *instantiates* them:

```
class Cash {
  public Cash(int dollars) {
    //...
  }
}
Cash five = new Cash(5);
```

This is different from what we call the Factory Pattern, but only because this `new` operator in Java is not as powerful as it could be. The only thing you can use it for is to make an instance—an object. If we ask class `Cash` to make a new object, we get a new object. There is no check for whether similar objects already exist and can be reused, there are no parameters that would modify the behavior of `new`, etc.

`new` is a primitive control for a factory of objects. In C++, there is also a `delete` operator that allows us to delete an object from the factory. In Java and many other "more advanced" languages, unfortunately, we don't have that. In C++, we can ask a factory to make an object for us, use it, and then ask the same factory to destroy it:

```
class Cash {
public:
  public Cash(int dollars);
}
Cash five = new Cash(5); // making an object
cout << five;
delete five; // destroying it
```

In Ruby, this idea of "a class as a factory" is most properly expressed in the following way:

```
class Cash
  def initialize(dollars)
    # ...
  end
end
Cash five = Cash.new(5)
```

`new` is a static method of class `Cash`, and when it's called, the class obtains control and makes object `five` for us. This object encapsulates number `5` and behaves like an integer.

Thus, a well-known Factory Pattern is a more powerful alternative to operator `new`, but conceptually they are the same. A class is a factory of objects. A class makes objects, keeps track of them, destroys them when necessary, etc. Most of these features, in most languages, are implemented by the runtime engine, not the code in the class, but it doesn't really matter. What we see on the surface is a class that can give us objects when we ask for them. You may wonder, what about utility classes, which don't have any objects. We will talk more about them later, in Section 3.2.3.

The Factory Pattern, in Java, works like an extension to the `new` operator. It makes it more flexible and powerful, by adding an extra logic in front of it. For example:

```
class Shapes {
  public Shape make(String name) {
    if (name.equals("circle")) {
      return new Circle();
    }
    if (name.equals("rectangle")) {
      return new Rectangle();
    }
    throw new IllegalArgumentException("not found");
  }
}
```

This is a typical factory in Java that helps us instantiate objects, using textual names of their types. In the end, we still use the `new` operator. My point is that conceptually, there is not much difference between Factory Pattern and `new` operator. In a perfect OOP language this functionality would be available in the `new` operator. I want you to think of a class as a warehouse of objects, which we can get from there when needed and return when not needed any more.

Sometimes a class is explained as a template of an object. This is absolutely wrong, because this definition makes a class a passive, brainless listing of code that is simply being copied somewhere when the time comes. Even though it may technically look like this for you, try not to *think* like this. A class is a *factory* of objects, period. By the way, I'm not promoting the Factory Pattern here. I'm actually not a big fan of it, although it is technically a valid concept. I'm saying that we should think about a class as an active manager of objects. We may also call it a storage unit or warehouse—a place where we get our objects and where we return them back.

Actually, having in mind that an object is a living creature, his class is his mother. That would be the most accurate metaphor.

Now, back to the main subject of this section—the problem of how to choose a good name for the class. There are basically two approaches: the right way and the wrong way. The wrong one would be to look at what our class objects are *doing* and give their class a name based on functionality. For example, here is a class named with this thinking in mind:

```
class CashFormatter {
  private int dollars;
  CashFormatter(int dlr) {
    this.dollars = dlr;
  }
  public String format() {
    return String.format("$ %d", this.dollars);
  }
}
```

When I have an object of class `CashFormatter`, what does it do for me? It formats dollar amounts to text. We should call it a formatter, right? Isn't that obvious?...

You probably noticed that I didn't call this `CashFormatter` a "he." This is because it is not an object I would respect. It is not something I can anthropomorphize and treat as a respectful citizen in my code.

This naming principle is very wrong and very popular. I encourage you not to follow this way of thinking. The name of a class should not originate from the functionality that its objects expose! Instead, a class should be named by what he *is*, not what he *does*. This `CashFormatter` must be renamed to `Cash` or `USDCash` or `CashInUSD`, etc. Method `format()` should be renamed to `usd()`. For example:

22

```
class Cash {
  private int dollars;
  Cash(int dlr) {
    this.dollars = dlr;
  }
  public String usd() {
    return String.format("$ %d", this.dollars);
  }
}
```

In other words, objects must be characterized by their capabilities. What I am is manifested by what I can do, not by my attributes, like my height, weight, or color.

The evil ingredient here is the "-er" suffix.

There are many examples of classes named like this, and all of them have that "-er" suffix, including Manager, Controller, Helper, Handler, Writer, Reader, Converter, Validator ("-or" is also evil), Router, Dispatcher, Observer, Listener, Sorter, Encoder, and Decoder. All these names are wrong. I'm sure you've seen many of them before. Here are a few counter examples: `Target`, `EncodedText`, `DecodedData`, `Content`, `SortedLines`, `ValidPage`, `Source`, etc.

The rule has exceptions though. Some English nouns have -er suffix, which originally was placed there in order to indicate that these nouns were performers of activities, but that was long time ago. For example, computer or user. We don't think anymore about a user as of something that is literally "using" something. It's more like a person who our system interacts with. We don't understand computer as something that "computes", instead it's an electronic device that is, well, a computer. But there are not so many exceptions like that.

An object is not a connector between his outside world and his inner world. An object is not a collection of procedures we can call in order to manipulate the data encapsulated inside him. Absolutely not! Instead, an object is a representative of his encapsulated data. See the difference?

A *connector* is not respected, because it just passes information through without actually being strong or smart enough to modify it or do something on its own. To the contrary, a *representative* is a self-sufficient entity who is capable of making his own decisions and acting on his own. Objects must be representatives, not connectors.

A class name that ends in "-er" tells us that this creature is not really an object but a collection of procedures that can manipulate some data. It is a procedural way of thinking that is inherited by many object-oriented developers from C, COBOL, Basic, and other languages. We are using Java and Ruby now, but we are still thinking in terms of data and procedures.

So, how do we name a class properly?

Look at what its objects will encapsulate and come up with a name for this group—simple as that. Let's say you have a list of numbers and an algorithm that tells you which number is prime. If you want to see a list of only prime numbers, don't call this class `Primer` or `PrimeFinder` or `PrimeChooser` or `PrimeHelper`. Instead, name him `PrimeNumbers` (this is Ruby, just for diversity):

```
class PrimeNumbers
  def initialize(origin)
    @origin = origin
  end
  def each
    @origin
      .select { |i| prime? i }
      .each { |i| yield i }
  end
  def prime?(x)
    # ...
  end
end
```

See what I mean? The class `PrimeNumbers` behaves like a list of numbers but returns only prime ones. Here is how we would design similar functionality in C, using a purely procedural style:

```
void find_prime_numbers(int* origin,
  int* primes, int size) {
  for (int i = 0; i < size; ++i) {
    primes[i] = (int) is_prime(origin[i]);
  }
}
```

Here, we have a procedure called `find_prime_numbers` that accepts two arrays of integers, goes through the first array to find all prime numbers, and marks their positions in the second array. There is no object involved. This is a purely *procedural* approach, and it is wrong. Well, it is still right in procedural languages, but we are in the OOP world.

This procedure is a connector between two pieces of data: an original list of numbers and a list of prime numbers. An object is something different. An object is not a connection; he is a representative of other objects and their combinations. In the example above, we create an object of class `PrimeNumbers` that behaves like a collection of numbers, but only prime numbers will be seen in the collection.

When your object is, in reality, the procedure `find_prime_numbers`, you are in trouble. An object is not supposed to work as a collection of procedures, even though technically he may look very similar. While the `PrimeNumbers` class encapsulates a list of numbers, it doesn't allow me to manage that list or find something in it. Instead, he says, "I am the list now!" When I need to do something with the list, I ask my object, and he decides what to do with my request. If he wants, he will get some data from the original list. If not, it's up to him.

`PrimeNumbers` *is* a list of numbers, not a bunch of methods that can help me manipulate the list. He is a *list*!

Let's summarize this section: When it's time to give a name to a new class, think what he *is*, not what he *does*. He is a list, and he can pick an element by number. He is an SQL record, and he can fetch a single cell as an integer. He is a pixel, and he can change his color. He is a file, and he can read his contents from the disc. He is an encoding algorithm, and he can encode. He is an HTML document, and he can be rendered.

What I do and who I am are two different things.

Also, yet another bad class name is the one that ends with `Util` or `Utils`. They are so called "utility classes" and will be discussed in Section 3.2.3.

1.2 Make one constructor primary

Discuss at http://goo.gl/brqhYS

Ctor is short for "constructor"; that's what they call them in C++, and I will do the same here, for brevity. So, a ctor is an entry point to a new object. It accepts some arguments, does something with them, and prepares the object to perform his duties:

```
class Cash {
  private int dollars;
  Cash(int dlr) {
    this.dollars = dlr;
  }
}
```

There is only one ctor in this example and the only thing it does is encapsulate the number of dollars in a private integer property, `dollars`. If you design your classes right, as explained in further chapters, they will have many ctors and just a few methods. That's right. You will have more ctors than methods in your classes. I'm aware that not all languages allow us to have many constructors in a class, due to the absence of a method overloading feature. We'll discuss that limitation in a minute.

Thus, two to three methods and five to 10 ctors. That is what a perfect class, in my opinion, should look like. Of course, it is not an exact science and these numbers are just made up. We'll discuss the amount of public methods in Section 3.1. My point here is that a cohesive and robust class will have a small number of methods and a rather big number of ctors.

Actually, the more ctors you have, the better—and the more convenient your classes are for me, their user. I want to be able to construct an instance of `Cash` in many different ways. For example:

```
new Cash(30);
new Cash("$29.95");
new Cash(29.95d);
new Cash(29.95f);
new Cash(29.95, "USD");
```

All of these statements should create the same object—the same in terms of its behavior. The greater the number of ctors, the more flexibility you give me, your client, to use your classes. On the contrary, the more methods your class exposes, the more difficult it is for me to use it. A large number of methods leads to a lack of focus and a violation of the Single Responsibility Principle, which we'll discuss in Section 3.1. A large number of ctors translates to flexibility.

As a user of `Cash`, I'm getting extra flexibility because I don't need to do class casting or parsing when I have my number in, say, text format. `Cash` is making this work for me. I have a text—here is a ctor for it. I have a double number—another ctor is there. Thanks to that flexibility, I write less code and less frequently duplicate myself. To the contrary, having many public methods is a bad idea, as it reduces flexibility.

The main job of a ctor is to initialize encapsulated properties using the arguments provided. My recommendation is to place this initialization into only one ctor and call it a "primary" one. Then, let all other ctors, called "secondary" ctors, call this primary one. For example:

```
class Cash {
  private int dollars;
  Cash(float dlr) {
    this((int) dlr);
  }
  Cash(String dlr) {
    this(Cash.parse(dlr));
  }
  Cash(int dlr) {
    this.dollars = dlr;
  }
}
```

I always try to place the primary ctor last in my code, after all secondary ones, just like in the example above. Mostly, for maintainability reasons. When I open a class created half a year ago, with ten constructors, I don't want to search for the primary one, reading them all. Instead, I just scroll down to the last one, which is always the primary.

There are two secondary ctors and one primary. The primary initializes `this.dollars` with the integer argument passed to it. Secondary ones prepare the integer argument for it, parsing or converting from other formats. In one of the ctors, I'm referring to a private static method `Cash.parse()`, which is parsing the text to convert it into integer. It's done this way because Java doesn't allow us to do anything before calling `this()`. In C++, we would not need this trick.

What is the point of this "one primary, many secondary" principle? It mostly helps avoid code duplication and make the design cleaner, which means higher maintainability. Here is how we would write the same class without this principle in mind:

```
class Cash {
  private int dollars;
  Cash(float dlr) { // wrong!
    this.dollars = (int) dlr;
  }
  Cash(String dlr) { // wrong!
    this.dollars = Cash.parse(dlr);
  }
  Cash(int dlr) {
    this.dollars = dlr;
  }
}
```

Now, let's say we want to make sure that dollar amount is always positive. We have to place the validation into three different places, in three ctors. In the first example above, with a single primary and two secondary ctors, the validation would be added to a single place and that's it.

Unfortunately, not all "object-oriented" languages support *method overloading*—which is what the technology of declaring methods or ctors with the same name but different arguments is called. For example, Ruby and PHP don't support method overloading. For some reason, they are still called object-oriented languages. I'm not joking here. Method overloading is a fundamental and very important feature of OOP. It seriously improves the readability of code, by making it semantically close to the business language. For example, the code would be much cleaner if we have two methods `content(File)` and `content(File,Charset)`, instead of `content(File)` and `contentInCharset(File,Charset)`.

Nevertheless, even in those languages, you still want to make your ctors flexible and multi-purpose. Well, your first thought should be to quit using them and migrate to Java, C++, or something similar that's powerful enough to be called an OOP language. If that's not possible (for example, it is JavaScript and there is no better alternative), use maps of arguments. This is PHP 5.4:

```
class Cash {
  private $_dollars;
  public function __construct($args) {
    if (is_int($args)) {
      $this->_dollars = $args;
    } else if (array_key_exists('float', $args)) {
      $this->__construct(intval($args['float']));
    } else if (array_key_exists('iso', $args)) {
      $this->__construct(
        parse_dollars($args['iso'])
      );
    } else {
      throw new Exception('can\'t initialize');
    }
  }
}
new Cash(30);
new Cash(['float' => 29.95]);
new Cash(['iso' => 'USD 29.95']);
```

The code looks much more verbose and less readable than in Java, but that's the best we can do. However, you see that there is the same principle is used—we initialize only in one place. All other places simply prepare the arguments and send them to that final primary place. Calling `__construct` method in PHP is a bad practice, but in this case it's acceptable. That is because this is the only option we have.

You can probably do some other magic in those overloading-free languages, but the main principle remains the same: initialization of internal properties happens only in one place. All other "places" simply prepare the arguments, reformat them, parse them, transform them, etc.

As in all other recommendations in this book, the main point is maintainability. This principle will help you reduce the complexity of code and avoid duplication—the two biggest enemies of maintainability.

1.3 Keep constructors code-free

Discuss at http://goo.gl/DCMFDY

We have a class with a primary ctor that accepts all necessary arguments. These arguments are enough to initialize the state of a new object. It's obvious, right? Since this ctor is the only entry point into the object initialization process, the provided collection of arguments is complete—nothing is missed and nothing is redundant. Now, the question that arises is what we can and can't do with this set of arguments. How do we manipulate them?

The rule of thumb here is "don't touch the arguments." Let's see a counterexample first. This code touches its only argument during object initialization:

```
class Cash {
  private int dollars;
  Cash(String dlr) {
    this.dollars = Integer.parseInt(dlr);
  }
}
```

Here, I want to encapsulate an integer while text is provided as an argument for the ctor. I need to convert the text to an integer, and I'll do this conversion right inside the ctor. Seems simple and obvious, doesn't it? Maybe, but it's a very *wrong* approach.

The initialization of an object must be "code-free" and must not touch the arguments. Instead, it must wrap them, if necessary, or encapsulate them in a raw form. Here is an example of the same code that doesn't "touch" the text:

```
class Cash {
  private Number dollars;
  Cash(String dlr) {
    this.dollars = new StringAsInteger(dlr);
  }
}
class StringAsInteger implements Number {
  private String source;
  StringAsInteger(String src) {
    this.source = src;
  }
  int intValue() {
    return Integer.parseInt(this.source);
  }
}
```

See the difference? In the first example, the conversion from text to a number happens right at the moment of object initialization. In the second example, it is delayed until the moment when an object of class `Cash` is actually used.

Of course, according to the principle discussed in the previous Section, the class `Cash` must have two ctors, one primary and one secondary:

```
class Cash {
  private Number dollars;
  Cash(String dlr) { // secondary
    this(new StringAsInteger(dlr));
  }
  Cash(Number dlr) { // primary
    this.dollars = dlr;
  }
}
```

On the surface, the instantiation of `Cash` looks exactly the same in both cases:

```
Cash five = new Cash("5");
```

However, in the first example, the `five` object encapsulates a number five, while in the second example, it encapsulates an instance of class `StringAsInteger` that *looks like* a `Number`. I just invented this class `StringAsInteger` right here. It doesn't exist in Java. As I already mentioned, Java is not really a true object-oriented language, which is why I sometimes have to make things up. Treat these examples as pseudo-code. But this doesn't mean that my recommendations are abstract and impractical. Instead, this means that not all of them are directly applicable to the software you're writing right now. Our goal here in this book is, first of all, to change our mindset and our understanding of OOP. The second goal is to give practical examples and apply our new mindset to the code we write. Unfortunately, the second goal is not always easy to achieve.

In a true object-oriented approach, instantiation is when we *compose* smaller objects into a larger one. The only reason for this process is that we need a new entity that obeys a new contract.

Look at our example with the `five` object of type `Cash`. What was wrong with a text object `"5"`? Why did we need to create an object of class `Cash`? Why couldn't we work with `"5"`? Because it didn't expose the methods we needed. It didn't work by the contract we needed. That's why we had to create a new object of a different type. We built `five` of type `Cash`. He doesn't work by `String` contract anymore; he works by some other contract. For example, he exposes method `cents()`.

We created him, but didn't ask him to work for us yet!

The first step is to instantiate an object; the second step is to allow him to work for us. These two steps should not overlap. A ctor should not ask its arguments to do anything, because the ctor itself wasn't asked to do anything yet. In other words, a ctor should be code-free. It should only contain assignment statements. In terms of C++, its body should always be empty. For example:

```
class Cash {
public:
  Cash(const string& txt):
    dollars(new StringAsInteger(txt)) {
    // the body is empty, always
  }
private:
  int dollars;
}
```

There are a few purely technical reasons for this recommendation. First of all, code-free ctors make your code faster... because they are easier to optimize for performance. Here is an example that will look slower at first glance but is indeed faster:

```
class StringAsInteger implements Number {
  private String text;
  public StringAsInteger(String txt) {
    this.text = txt;
  }
  public int intValue() {
    return Integer.parseInt(this.text);
  }
}
```

It looks like we are going to run text to integer parsing on every call of `intValue()`, right? Indeed, that's true. This code will parse twice:

```
Number num = new StringAsInteger("123");
num.intValue(); // first parsing
num.intValue(); // second parsing
```

How, then, can it be faster than this, you may ask:

```
class StringAsInteger implements Number {
  private int num;
  public StringAsInteger(String txt) {
    this.num = Integer.parseInt(txt);
  }
  public int intValue() {
    return this.num;
  }
}
```

This code is indeed more effective, since it parses only once—during object initialization. Then, on every consecutive call to `intValue()`, the object just returns the encapsulated integer. So, what is the point?

Here is the point. The second example, where the parsing happens in the ctor, is not optimizable. The parsing will happen every time we make an object. We can't control it. Even if, in some situations, we don't need to call `intValue()`, our CPU will spend time parsing. Consider this example:

```
Number five = new StringAsInteger("5");
if (/* something is wrong */) {
  throw new Exception("some problem");
}
five.intValue();
```

As you can see, we parsed `"5"` first and then realized that we didn't need it! And we have no way to prevent this from happening. Every time we construct an object, it immediately proceeds with the arguments we give it. It happens without our approval, and it happens always. To the contrary, if we encapsulate the arguments the way they are passed and process them later, *on demand*, we give our users the freedom to decide when this should happen.

When the user wants to prevent multiple parsings from happening, he or she can always create a *decorator* that will cache the result of the parsing right after the first call:

```
class CachedNumber implements Number {
  private Number origin;
  private Collection<Integer> cached =
    ArrayList<>(1);
  public CachedNumber(Number num) {
    this.origin = num;
  }
  public int intValue() {
    if (this.cached.isEmpty()) {
      this.cached.add(this.origin.intValue());
    }
    return this.cached.get(0);
  }
}
```

I'm using `ArrayList` in order to avoid `null`, which is a very bad thing in OOP. We will discuss this later in Sections 4.1 and 3.3.

This is a rather primitive implementation of caching, but I hope you got the idea. Then, this caching decorator is used to wrap an object we want to make more effective:

```
Number num = new CachedNumber(
  new StringAsInteger("123")
);
num.intValue(); // first parsing
num.intValue(); // no parsing here
```

The beauty of this solution is that it's very controllable and transparent. The instantiation of an object doesn't do anything except *build* an object, while his methods do the actual job. Moreover, we control it all! We optimize while the object works.

Thus, by making ctors code-free, we make our objects more controllable and transparent for their users. We make them easier to understand and reuse. They work only when being asked to and don't do anything until that very moment. They are very "lazy"—in a good way.

There could be situations when it's absolutely clear that we have to do all manipulations only once. In these situations, why can't we do this in the ctor? We can, but I would still caution against it, mostly for the sake of uniformity. You don't know what will happen with this class in the future and how much will be changed after the next refactoring. Placing any manipulations into the ctor we will make that refactoring much more difficult. The author of refactoring will have to move manipulations into the methods. Only then will the author be able to start making real changes.

I've tried to find a second technical reason for this recommendation of keeping ctors code-free, but can't. It appears the one I explained above is the only reason—lightweight ctors make objects faster due to a more configurable and transparent usage. That's it.

Moreover, if you look at properly designed object-oriented software, you should see something like this:

```
App app = new App(new Data(), new Screen());
app.run();
```

This is a very abstract example, but I hope you get the idea.

First, we build an app, then we pass control to it. While we build the app, it doesn't do anything. It doesn't connect to the database, it doesn't open any ports, it doesn't process any data. It just creates all objects inside it and gets them ready to work. Then, we call `run()`, which allows all objects to do their job when and where they are necessary.

All your objects, from the top-level `App` to the lowest-level `StringAsInteger`, must be designed with this thinking in mind—their primary ctors must be code-free.

Chapter 2

Education

The sections in this book are grouped into chapters rather artificially, but still there is some logic behind it. In this chapter, we'll discuss a few principles of making an object ready for interaction with other objects. We'll send him to school and give him a few good lessons on how to behave.

Here is a summary of all the advice you will read in the next few sections: An object has to be *small*. A small object is an elegant and maintainable object. There can be no excuse in OOP for a class of 1,000 lines. Unfortunately, keeping an object small is easier said than done. How can we make an object small if there are so many functionality requirements? Bear with me. A few practical recommendations follow.

2.1 Encapsulate as little as possible

Remember, it's all about maintainability. Everything I've written about in this book directly affects the complexity of your code, which directly affects its *maintainability*. The higher the complexity, the lower the maintainability, which leads to the waste of time, money, and customer satisfaction[1]. I'm sure we are on the same page here.

With this in mind, I recommend you encapsulate *four* objects or less. If you need to encapsulate more, there is something wrong with the class, and it needs refactoring. No exceptions. Four or fewer. I'm just making this number up, there is no scientific proof behind it, but I will explain why four in the next few pages.

Encapsulated objects, all together, are also known as the "state" or "identity" of the object. For example:

```
class Cash {
  private Integer digits;
  private Integer cents;
  private String currency;
}
```

Here, we encapsulate three objects. All three of them together identify objects of class `Cash`, which means that any two objects encapsulating the same dollars, cents, and currency are equal to each other. Yes, this is a technically invalid statement in the Java world, but that's just a flaw of Java design, in my opinion. Here is how I think the object paradigm should be implemented in a purely object-oriented language:

---

[1] I don't have any statistics to prove that claim, but it sounds very logical to me. If you know any of research in this field, please let me know and I'll add it in the next edition of the book.

```
Cash x = new Cash(29, 95, "USD");
Cash y = new Cash(29, 95, "USD");
assert x.equals(y);
assert x == y;
```

In Java, as well as in C++, the identity of an object is separate from its state. These two objects, `x` and `y`, have the same state but different identities. They are not equal to each other, as far as the `==` operator is concerned, and their default implementation of `equals()` also states they are not the same.

It's a flaw in Java design, inherited from C++. As far as I understand, an "object" in OOP is an aggregation of other objects that work together to produce high level behavior. A book is an aggregation of pages, a cover, and an ISBN, while a bookshelf is an aggregation of books and a title. A car is an aggregation of wheels, an engine, and a windshield, while a garage is an aggregation of cars and an address. An employee is an aggregation of a name, age, and salary, while a department is an aggregation of employees, a name, and a manager. These are very primitive examples, but they demonstrate that without encapsulated objects, an object doesn't and can't exist—because he is nothing without his parts.

In Java, however, an object can exist without parts and without being equal to an exact duplicate that also has no parts. This goes against common sense. But there is sense in Java for that. In Java and almost all other OOP languages, an object is just a set of data with methods attached to it. It's like a shell where some data can be stored. Whether or not it stores data, one shell is different from others, despite comparing duplicate objects:

```
Object x = new Object();
Object y = new Object();
assert x.equals(y); // fails
```

This is a perfectly valid piece of code that shows how two objects are just two shells with no data inside. Of course, they are not equal to each other because they are different shells. That's how Java sees objects. And it's terribly wrong.

An object must not exist without a state, and the state must be his identity.

Since we agree that all encapsulated objects are part of an object's identity, we have to decide how many of them are *reasonable* to encapsulate. As I said above, up to four is a reasonable number. Why four? Here is my justification.

The identity of an object is basically its coordinates in the universe. My identity is my name and my date of birth. Using these two properties, you can find me in the entire universe (well, provided that this time and the Earth are the only existing coordinate spaces). My car has a make, a model, and a year of manufacture. These three properties uniquely identify it in the universe. I can give you more examples, but the point is that having more than four coordinates is just counterintuitive. It is just too difficult to understand in our current way of thinking about objects in the universe. One of my reviewers gave me a counter example here. He said that even if he and his neighbour have cars of the same make, model and year, they are still different cars. That's true, but that's because in this counter example the car is a much more complex thing than in my object-oriented example above. Of course, if our object is referring to a real car from a real world, it must have way more coordinates and attributes to identify itself in a unique way. But these attributes will be grouped into other objects, which all together will organize a tree of objects. Say, a car will encapsulate a type and a Vehicle Identification Number (VIN). A type will encapsulate a make, a model, and a year. Thus, we'll have a small tree of objects.

Of course, I've seen classes encapsulate dozens of objects. This is absolutely wrong. Don't do this. Four is the maximum. If you need more, break your class down into small ones.

And, by the way, to resolve that Java flaw, I recommend you stay away from the `==` operator and always override the `equals()` method[1].

---

[1] To make things simple, I utilize `@EqualsAndHashCode` from the Lombok project.

2.2 Encapsulate something at the very least

Discuss at http://goo.gl/QE9aXg

Another extreme is an object that encapsulates nothing at all. For example (this algorithm is wrong, but it's not important here):

```
class Year {
  int read() {
    return System.currentTimeMillis()
      / (1000 * 60 * 60 * 24 * 30 * 12) + 1970;
  }
}
```

An instance of this class will encapsulate nothing, which means that all objects of class `Year` will be equal to each other, considering what we just discussed in Section 2.1, right? This design is also wrong. Encapsulating too much is a bad idea, but encapsulating nothing is also not the way to go.

A class without properties is very similar to a static method, which is a terrible thing in object-oriented programming (Section 3.2). Such a class has no state and no identity, just behavior. What is wrong with that, you ask? The answer is simple. In pure OOP, without static methods (Section 3.2) and with a strict separation of instantiation and execution (Section 3.6), this would technically not be possible.

The instantiation should be isolated from execution, which means exactly this: operator `new` is allowed only inside constructors. More about that in Section 3.6. For now, let's just assume that in a true object-oriented design, the operator `new` is allowed only inside ctors.

Now, look at the class above. Its method `read()` uses a static method from utility class `System`. In pure OOP, we would not have static methods at all and would not be able to make this call. Instead, we would have to make an instance of some class, which would retrieve the value of the system clock. This is how our design would look:

```
class Year {
  private Millis millis;
  Year(Millis msec) {
    this.millis = msec;
  }
  int read() {
    return this.millis.read()
      / (1000 * 60 * 60 * 24 * 30 * 12) + 1970;
  }
}
```

We have to encapsulate something unless our object is very close to "nothing." By "nothing", I mean a creature without any coordinates in the Universe. Only such an entity would not have anything to encapsulate, since it's the only one and it doesn't need any other entities to survive and position itself. To the contrary, any object that does something co-exists with other objects and utilizes them. He has to encapsulate them in order to identify himself. This may sound rather abstract and philosophical. That's exactly how it should sound. There is no practical reasoning for that. We definitely can create an object that encapsulates nothing. There are multiple examples for that. But philosophically speaking, it's wrong and that's why it's wrong in practice.

Also, let's look at this problem from another point of view. As we discussed in Section 2.1, encapsulated state is a unique identity of an object that positions him in the universe. If there are no encapsulated items, what are his coordinates? Yes, they're the entire universe:

```
class Universe {
}
```

This class may exist, but only once. Because there is only one Universe. I don't see any practical reason for its existence, though.

By the way, I've mentioned above that the design is "better", but not perfect. This is what a perfect object-oriented design would look like:

```
class Year {
  private Number num;
  Year(final Millis msec) {
    this.num = new Min(
      new Div(
        msec,
        new Mul(1000, 60, 60, 24, 30, 12)
      ),
      1970
    );
  }
  int read() {
    return this.num.intValue();
  }
}
```

Or like this:

```
class Year {
  private Number num;
  Year(final Millis msec) {
    this.num = msec.div(
        1000.mul(60).mul(60).mul(24).mul(30).mul(12)
    ).add(1970);
  }
  int read() {
    return this.num.intValue();
  }
}
```

But more about this later.

2.3 Always use interfaces

Discuss at http://goo.gl/vo9F2g

Now let's talk about the mission of an object in the world he is going to live in. As I mentioned above, an object is a living organism that communicates with other organisms and helps them do their work. They also help the object do his work. It's a very social, tight environment.

What I mean here is that objects are *coupled* to each other because they need each other. It's very good at the beginning, when we know exactly what each object has to do and which services he has to provide to other objects. But when the application starts to grow and the number of objects exceeds a few dozen, *tight coupling* between them becomes a serious problem. This problem affects maintainability. It's all about maintainability. Every section in this book aims to encourage you to care about maintainability more than anything else, including performance.

In order to make our entire application maintainable, we have to do the best we can to *decouple* objects. Technically, this means that I can modify one object without modifying the others that interact with it. The best instrument for this is *interfaces*. For example:

```
interface Cash {
  Cash multiply(float factor);
}
```

This is the interface. In other words, it's a *contract* that our object must obey in order to communicate with other objects. Here is how:

```
class DefaultCash implements Cash {
  private int dollars;
  DefaultCash(int dlr) {
    this.dollars = dlr;
  }
  @Override
  Cash multiply(float factor) {
    return new DefaultCash(this.dollars * factor);
  }
}
```

Now, when I need to use cash value, I rely on the contract instead of the actual implementation:

```
class Employee {
  private Cash salary;
}
```

This `Employee` class doesn't really care how interface `Cash` is implemented. It's not interested in how the method `multiply()` really works. It simply doesn't know how it works. This literally means that interface `Cash` helps us decouple class `Employee` and class `DefaultCash`. Now I can change `DefaultCash`, or even replace it with something else. The `Employee` doesn't care.

I'm sure all of this is obvious, but here is my suggestion: make sure that *all* public methods in your class implement some interfaces. A properly designed class must not have any public methods that don't implement at least one interface. In other words, this is not an acceptable design:

```
class Cash {
  public int cents() {
    // something
  }
}
```

This `cents()` method does not override anything, and it's wrong. Because this design encourages its users (other classes) to couple to the class tightly. Objects of other classes will use `Cash.cents()` directly, and there won't be any possibility in the future to replace the implementation with a new one.

On a more philosophical note, a class is there only because someone needs his service. This service must be documented somewhere—it's a contract, an interface. Moreover, there has to be a competition between providers of the service. This is what multiple classes implementing the same interface are about. And each competitor must be easily replaceable with another one. This is what *loose coupling* is about.

You may say that even though we don't couple classes directly any more, we do via interfaces. A class must implement an interface in order to be understood and used by another class. We can't change the interface without making immediate changes to all classes that implement it and all classes that use it. That's true. This coupling is still there and there is no way to get rid of it. Actually, this coupling is not a bad thing. It allows us to keep the entire system in a stable state. We can't break it by accidental changes to one part of it, where the other part doesn't know about the changes. Interfaces, as contracts between parts, help us keep the entire environment organized.

2.4 Choose method names carefully

We've already discussed how to name a class in Section 1.1. Now it's time to name methods properly. I suggest this simple rule of thumb: builders are *nouns*, manipulators are *verbs*[1].

Builders are what I call methods that build something and return a new object. Builders always return something. They never return `void`, and their names are always nouns. For example:

```
int pow(int base, int power);
float speed();
Employee employee(int id);
String parsedCell(int x, int y);
```

Pay attention to that last method, `parsedCell()`. It's not just a noun, but a noun with an adjective in front of it. That doesn't change the principle; it only makes the name more descriptive. It's still a noun, but with more information. It's not just a cell, but a parsed cell. We should probably expect this method to return a cell that has transformed its contents somehow.

I call a *manipulator* a method that makes modifications to the real-world entity being abstracted by an object. It always returns `void`, and its names are always verbs. For example:

```
void save(String content);
void put(String key, Float value);
void remove(Employee emp);
void quicklyPrint(int id);
```

Pay attention to the last method, `quicklyPrint()`. It's a verb

---

[1] This idea is very similar to the one suggested by Bertrand Meyer in his book *Object Oriented Software Construction* (Prentice Hall, 2nd edition, 1997), where he proposes to divide object's methods into two sharply separated categories: queries and commands.

with an adverb in front of it. The key element here is the verb
"print", while "quickly" just explains it, giving us more
information about the context and the purpose of the method.

You may give your own names to these builders and
manipulators, but try to keep this principle intact: builders build
and manipulators manipulate. And there is nothing in between.
There should not be any methods that manipulate and return
something, nor build and manipulate at the same time. Let me
give a few bad examples:

```
// returns total bytes saved
int save(String content);
// returns TRUE if map was modified
boolean put(String key, Float value);
// saves speed and returns previous value
float speed(float val);
```

The design of method `save()` is bad because it is a manipulator.
It "saves", but at the same time, it returns `int` as if it was a
builder. We should either return `void` or rename it to something
like `bytesSaved()`.

The same problem occurs with method `put()`, which works as a
manipulator, but returns `boolean` as a builder. The only
solution here is to return `void`. But we want to know whether
the value was changed for the given key! In that case, we have to
change the entire design of the class and, for example, return an
instance of `PutOperation`. This would have a manipulator
`save()` and a success/failure status via `success()`. The
method `speed()` saves the value and also returns the previous
one. Yet another example of a bad design, because at the same
time, it is a builder and a manipulator. We can fix that similarly
to the previous example, by creating a class `SaveSpeed`, which

would have two methods, one for saving the speed and another one for returning its previous value.

We'll discuss "setters" and "getters" later, in Section 3.5. Here, I believe, it's already obvious that names that start with `get` are just wrong. Well, because "get" is a verb but getters are basically builders, since they are supposed to return something. So, this is my first argument against "getters."

Now, I think I owe you an explanation for this idea. There are a few arguments in its favor.

2.4.1 Builders are nouns

First, it's wrong to name a method as a verb if it returns something. Such a name goes against the idea of object thinking. When I stop in at a bakery, I don't say "cook me a brownie" or "brew me a cup of coffee." I'd say, "I'd like a brownie" or "I'd like to have a cup of coffee." If I said "cook me" or "brew me" something, it would sound rather offensive. I should not care how exactly that brownie is made or how that cup of coffee is brewed. How the bakery makes them is its business. I have demand for an object—a brownie or a cup of coffee. They can satisfy my demand. How exactly this happens inside the bakery is none of my business. Here is the bakery:

```
class Bakery {
  Food cookBrownie();
  Drink brewCupOfCoffee(String flavor);
}
```

These two methods are not actually methods of an object. They are *procedures*. Their naming tells us that we ought to pay no respect to the bakery as a self-sufficient and self-managed object, and just tell it what to do for us. This is a procedural approach, not an object-oriented one. This is how these two procedures would be designed in C, for example:

```
Food* cook_brownie() {
  // cook that brownie
  // and return it
}
Drink* brew_cup_of_coffee(char* flavor) {
  // brew a cup of coffee
  // and return it
}
```

There is no bakery involved. We just have two pieces of machine instructions in C syntax, and we call them. We call them functions in C, but they are actually procedures because they have very little to do with functional programming as well. We ask the computer to run those instructions for us and return the result. We are thinking like a computer, not like an object. We don't trust the bakery, so we tell it to "go and brew the damn coffee" instead of asking for a cup of coffee with a certain flavor and then just entrusting the establishment with the result, no matter what it is.

I don't want to sound too philosophical, but this naming subject is indeed very abstract and conceptual. A properly named method helps its users better understand what the object is designed for, what his mission is, what the purpose of his existence is, and what the meaning of life is for him. An improper method name may ruin the entire idea of an object and encourage its users to treat him as a bag of data and a collection of procedures. It's a very typical mistake that is repeatedly made by OOP libraries, SDKs, APIs, etc. An object is a *living organism* who knows how to perform his duties and wants to be respected.

He wants to work by the contract, not just follow instructions. There is a big difference. Just like us, programmers, right?

That's why when the name of the method is a verb, it's basically telling the object "what to do." And asking an object to "build" something is not a polite and respectful way to work with him. Just request what you need to be built, and let him decide how to build it. All of these names are wrong:

```
InputStream load(URL url);
String read(File file);
int add(int x, int y);
```

They should be replaced with:

```
InputStream stream(URL url);
String content(File file);
int sum(int x, int y);
```

Pay attention to the fact that instead of `add(x,y)`, I'm suggesting you use `sum(x,y)`. It may look like a small and unimportant change, but it really makes a big difference in your thinking. We don't ask our object to add x to y. Instead, we ask him to produce the sum of the two and return a new object. Will he really find the sum? I don't know. Maybe. All I know is that the result will look like the sum of x and y. Again, I'm not telling my object what to do, I'm just asking for a result that must obey a certain contract—be an integer number. In Java and many other languages, a number is not an object, but a scalar. That's just a defect in those languages. In a true object-oriented environment everything is an object, especially strings, numbers, boolean values, bits, and bytes.

This is the first argument and the first use case. We are getting something from an object, or in other words, asking an object to build something for us. Now, let's discuss the second argument and the second use case, when we ask the object to do some manipulation for us.

2.4.2 Manipulators are verbs

An object is a representative of a real-world entity. An object of class `File` represents a file on disk, an object of class `Pixel` represents a pixel on the screen, and an instance of class `Integer` represents four bytes of RAM (Surprised? We'll discuss that in detail in Section 3.4).

When we need to manipulate a real-world entity, we ask the object to do it for us. For example:

```
class Pixel {
  void paint(Color color);
}
Pixel center = new Pixel(50, 50);
center.paint(new Color("red"));
```

We ask object `center` to paint a pixel on the screen, located at the `50x50` coordinates. We don't expect anything to be built. We just want to make a modification to the world, and the object is a representative of that for us. Now, you may ask how this is not a procedure. It is named as a verb, and it basically directs an object to do something for us. Yes, it's a valid question, but the key difference is the result returned.

The method `paint()` doesn't return a result. Using the same bakery metaphor, this is similar to asking a bartender to turn up the music. Will she make it louder? Maybe she will. Maybe not. Our request may just be ignored. It's never offensive or disrespectful, because we are not expecting anything back.

Imagine how this would sound otherwise—"Please turn up the music and tell me its volume level when you're done." That's exactly how a manipulator that returns a value looks. Very disrespectful.

Thus, the difference is in the return value. Only a builder is allowed to return a value, and its name must be a noun. When an object allows us to manipulate, the name has to be a verb, and there must be no return value.

I think it's possible to follow a less strict naming convention, provided you keep the main principle in mind. For example, when using a Builder Pattern, you can start method names with a `with` prefix:

```
class Book {
   Book withAuthor(String author);
   Book withTitle(String title);
   Book withPage(Page page);
}
```

Here, the name `withTitle` is just a short form of `bookWithTitle`. In order to avoid this `book` prefix in all methods, we can use just the `with` prefix. But the principle is still in place—these methods are builders, and their names are classified as nouns. By the way, I'm in general against this Builder Pattern, mostly because it encourages us to make bigger objects, which are inevitably less maintainable and way less cohesive than smaller ones. We use builders when we don't want to pass a large amount of arguments into ctors. That's where builders are helpful. But large amount of arguments is the problem in the first place. Instead of using builders, we should break our complex objects into smaller ones. Long story short, don't use builders.

2.4.3 Examples of both

Let's discuss a few practical examples of refactoring. Let's say we have a method that saves file content and returns the number of bytes actually saved:

```
class Document {
  int write(InputStream content);
}
```

It looks like a valid method, but it violates the principle I just described. It has to return `void`, but we need to know how many bytes were actually saved. What do we do? Just rename it to `bytesWritten()`? That would be wrong, because the purpose of the method is not to calculate bytes, but to actually write the content to the document.

The builders/manipulators naming principle actually tells us in this example that the method `write()` is doing too many things at the same time. It writes the data and counts the bytes. That's too complex for a single method. We can't give it a clean noun or verb name because its purpose is not clear enough. It's unfocused. Here is how I recommend we refactor it:

```
class Document {
  OutputPipe output();
}
class OutputPipe {
  void write(InputStream content);
  int bytes();
  long time();
}
```

As you see, method `output()` is a builder. It builds a new object of type `OutputPipe` that is ready to write the content (pay attention, I don't call it a "writer"). The content is not yet

60

written; we just have an object ready to perform this operation for us. Then, we call `write()` on the pipe, and it collects the data about this transaction. Now we can collect more information than just the number of bytes. We can collect the time of the transaction and many other things.

The designers of Go language made a big mistake, in my opinion. They made it possible to return multiple values from a single method, which encourages programmers to make methods even more complex and unfocused than in other languages. In Go, we would be able to declare method `write()` like this:

```
type Document struct {}
func (d Document) write(s Stream) (int, int) {}
```

This is how our code gets messy and maintainability decreases, while the whole purpose of OOP is to decrease complexity by isolation of concepts. The smaller the concept being isolated, the easier it is to understand and maintain. The concept in this case is "writing bytes to the document." The refactoring I proposed above isolates the concept in its own class called `OutputPipe`, while Go encourages me to stay in `Document` and make its method, `write()`, even more complex.

2.4.4 Boolean results

Wait, what about methods that return Boolean values? For example, take method `isEmpty()` in class `String`. How would you recommend naming it, you may ask. Or method `equals()` in `Object`. Or method `exists()` in `File`. There are many of them everywhere. According to the principle described above, all these names are wrong. But what is the alternative?

I think methods that return Boolean values are an exception to this rule. They are also builders, but for better readability, their names should be *adjectives*. For example:

```
boolean empty();
boolean readable();
boolean negative();
```

Prefix `is` is redundant and should not be used, but it should always be temporarily placed in front of the method name in order to ensure that it sounds right. I mean place it, read it, and use the name without the prefix. This mental exercise is required in order to avoid using verbs instead of adjectives. For example, here's what all these methods would sound like:

```
boolean empty();  // is empty
boolean readable();  // is readable
boolean negative();  // is negative
```

However, these methods will cause problems:

```
boolean equals(Object obj);
boolean exists();
```

This is mostly because "`isEquals`" and "`isExists`" don't sound right. Much better names would be `equalTo` and `present`, because "is equal to" and "is present" do sound right.

Why are Boolean methods an exception? Well, because Java and most other languages give it a special treatment in logical constructs. Say, we have class `String`, which has builder method `length()`. We add method `emptiness()`, which will return the status of the string—either it's empty or not. Then, use it like this:

```
if (name.emptiness() == true) {
  // do something
}
```

This reads correctly: "if emptiness of the name is true." However, we don't do that in Java. We use a shorter form of this comparison. We simply skip the `==true` part. That's why an adjective will sound nicer:

```
if (name.empty()) { // "if name is empty"
  // do something
}
```

Let me summarize this section. First, make sure you know the mission of your method. It's either a builder or a manipulator. It can't be both, ever. Then, name it with a noun if it's a builder, or with a verb if it's a manipulator. The only exception is a builder that returns a Boolean value. In this case, use an adjective. That's it.

2.5 Don't use public constants

Discuss at http://goo.gl/Q1Uoru

A public static final property, also known as a "constant", is a very popular mechanism for sharing data between objects. Yes, that's exactly what these constants are for—sharing data (or other objects). And this is what I'm strongly against. Objects should not share anything; they should instead be self-sufficient and very "closed." This sharing mechanism simply goes against the idea of encapsulation and the entire object-oriented way of thinking. Let's discuss this through an example. Say I have a method that writes some structured data to the `Writer` and terminates each line with a "new line":

```
class Records {
  private static final String EOL = "\r\n";
  void write(Writer out) {
    for (Record rec : this.all) {
      out.write(rec.toString());
      out.write(Records.EOL);
    }
  }
}
```

In this example, the static final property `EOL` is private and is used only inside the class `Records`. That is a perfectly valid situation. We just don't want to write `"\r\n"` every time we need it inside this class. Now let's say we have another class that is doing something very similar, but with different objects:

```
class Rows {
  private static final String EOL = "\r\n";
  void print(PrintStream pnt) {
    for (Row row : this.fetch()) {
      pnt.printf(
        "{ %s }%s", row, Rows.EOL
      );
    }
  }
}
```

There is different logic in this class, and it works with a completely different set of objects. These two classes, `Records` and `Rows`, are not connected by anything. They have nothing in common. However, they both define a private constant: `EOL`. Is this code duplication? Of course it is. How do we resolve it? How did we resolve it in C? We had the `#define` macro, which allowed us to define it once and reuse it everywhere:

```
#define EOL "\r\n"
```

However, we are not in C anymore. We have objects in OOP, and solving code duplication problems by means of public constants is a very incorrect approach. It is very procedural; that's why it's wrong. Here is how we could "solve" it in Java:

```
public class Constants {
   public static final String EOL = "\r\n";
}
```

How different is it from the `#define` C macro? Not much. They are both available in the global scope of visibility—every class may use them. I would actually say that the C macro is better, because it is *not* visible to everybody. It is visible only if you include a certain `.h` file where this macro is declared. In Java, class `Constants` is public, and that's why it's visible to literally all other classes in the class loader.

By introducing class `Constants`, we are "solving" the code duplication problem, because classes `Records` and `Rows` will use `Constants.EOL` instead of `Records.EOL` and `Rows.EOL`, respectively. They will not have to define this constant locally anymore. They will just "reuse" a publicly available one. The problem's solved, isn't it? Not at all!

By solving one problem, we introduced two bigger ones: 1) the introduction of *coupling* and 2) the loss of *cohesion*.

2.5.1 Introduction of coupling

First, the coupling problem. Here is how our class `Records` looks now:

```
class Records {
  void write(Writer out) {
    for (Record rec : this.all) {
      out.write(rec.toString());
      out.write(Constants.EOL); // here!
    }
  }
}
```

This is how `Rows` looks:

```
class Rows {
  void print(PrintStream pnt) {
    for (Row row : this.fetch()) {
      pnt.printf(
        "{ %s }", row, Constants.EOL // here!
      );
    }
  }
}
```

Now, they both depend on the same object, and these dependencies are *hard-coded*. There is no easy way to break them. We have three places where sections of code are coupled to each other and depend on each other: `Records.write()`, `Rows.print()`, and `Constants.EOL`. If I change the content of `Constants.EOL`, the behavior of two classes will change in an unpredictable way. Why unpredictable? Because when I change the value of `Constants.EOL`, I have no idea *how* this value is used. Maybe it's used for ending lines while printing. Or maybe it is used to end lines in an HTTP protocol, where changing these line endings is absolutely impossible due to a mandatory requirement of HTTP.

The object `Constants.EOL` remains alone in a global scope of visibility, without any semantic usage around it. We simply don't know how this object is used, in what context, and how the changes we may make will affect its users. We encourage its users to be coupled with it, which will eventually lead to a huge loss in maintainability. Remember, it's all about maintainability! When many objects use another object and we don't know how they use it—they are coupled to it very tightly.

When the constant is rather primitive, like this `EOL`, the problem is not that big because the semantics are rather clear. However, when the constant is more complex, the problem becomes more serious.

2.5.2 Loss of cohesion

By using public constants, our objects become less cohesive—in other words, less focused on solving their own specific problems. They have to *know* how to deal with the constants. They have to add their own *semantics* to those pretty dumb constants. Yes indeed, they are dumb. What does this `Constants.EOL` know about itself? Nothing. It is just a piece of text that doesn't even understand what it's for. It doesn't know its own mission and purpose. The meaning of life is not clear for this constant, philosophically speaking.

In order to add semantics, we have to write more code in classes `Records` and `Rows`. We have to wrap those primitive static constants in some code that will make their purpose more clear. But it's not the purpose of `Records` and `Rows`. They are designed to work with records or rows, not with line endings. They would be cohesive if they could outsource this job to someone—"I work with records and you help me deal with line endings." That would be a fair request, which would help our classes stay more cohesive.

So, what is the alternative? Here is what I'm suggesting to resolve the code duplication problem properly. We should not share data between objects. Instead, we should create *new classes* that help us share functionality. Again, not data but functionality! For example, we see that in both classes, we need to print lines that end with `EOL`. Let's create a class for that:

```
class EOLString {
  private final String origin;
  EOLString(String src) {
    this.origin = src;
  }
  @Override
  String toString() {
    return String.format("%s\r\n", origin);
  }
}
```

Now we can use it when necessary, like in `Records`:

```
class Records {
  void write(Writer out) {
    for (Record rec : this.all) {
      out.write(new EOLString(rec.toString()));
    }
  }
}
```

And in `Rows`:

```
class Rows {
  void print(PrintStream pnt) {
    for (Row row : this.fetch()) {
      pnt.print(
        new EOLString(
          String.format("{ %s }", row)
        )
      );
    }
  }
}
```

Now, the functionality that appends a suffix to the line is perfectly isolated in class `EOLString`. How exactly that suffix is added to the line is up to this class. In `Records` and `Rows`, we don't have that logic. We don't know how exactly a line gets a required suffix. All we know is that `EOLString` is responsible for that job.

You might say that now we are coupled with class `EOLString`, which is the same as being coupled with `Constants.EOL`, but it's not. Yes, we are coupled with `EOLString`, but this coupling doesn't degrade maintainability because it's a coupling *through a contract*, which means that it's breakable. There are two equally smart elements in this coupling—an object of class `Records` and an object of class `EOLString`. The latter works by the contract, and the semantics of the contract are encapsulated inside it.

Let's say that tomorrow we want to change our behavior depending on the platform we're currently working on. We don't want to use `"\r\n"` when running on Windows. We want to throw an exception in this situation. Our contract (interface) stays the same, but the behavior changes:

```
class EOLString {
  private final String origin;
  EOLString(String src) {
    this.origin = src;
  }
  String toString() {
    if (/* this is Windows */) {
      throw new IllegalStateException(
        "We're on Windows, can't use EOL, sorry"
      );
    }
    return String.format("%s\r\n", origin);
  }
}
```

Was it possible to do this with a public static literal? Not really.

Does this mean that for each public constant we should create a new class, which will encapsulate the semantics of this constant? Yes. Does this mean we may have hundreds of micro classes instead of hundreds of simple constant string literals? Yes. Won't this make our code more verbose and polluted by redundant micro classes? No. The more small classes you have, the cleaner the code—provided the small classes don't duplicate each other. This statement may sound not logical to you, let's stop here for a second. It's important. I do mean that the more classes you have in your application, the better its design and more maintainable it is. The best analogy here is with a language we speak. The more words you use in English, provided they are not just synonyms being used to impress the reader, the more readable your text is. To the contrary, if you put too much meaning in some words and reuse them frequently, the text becomes unreadable. Here is an example:

```
My cat likes to eat fish and drink milk.
```

Here is another example, which uses a bit less words:

```
My thing likes to eat that thing and
drink another thing.
```

We're overusing the word "thing", putting too much meaning into it. The reader should figure out what exactly that "thing" means in the first place, in the second and in the third ones. Instead, using "cat", "fish", and "milk" helps us digest the semantics faster. The same happens with classes, which are too big and too powerful. Sometimes, we simply don't know what that `java.io.File` means exactly, if it's used everywhere. It would be much more convenient to have `TextFile`, `JPGFile`, or

`TempFile`.

Let me give you another example. Every HTTP client I know, not only in Java, provides the possibility to change the HTTP request method in this way:

```
String body = new HttpRequest()
  .method("POST")
  .fetch();
```

Then, you have a collection of public static literals for the names of HTTP methods. In the end, your code looks similar to this:

```
String body = new HttpRequest()
  .method(HttpMethods.POST)
  .fetch();
```

That runs contrary to the spirit of OOP. Instead, it would be much better to create a number of simple classes that would represent those methods:

```
String body = new PostRequest(new HttpRequest())
  .fetch();
```

Now, `PostRequest` knows how to configure `HttpRequest` so it makes a `POST` request instead of a default `GET` one. The logic of this configuration, the *semantics* of the `"POST"` literal, is encapsulated inside a new class, `PostRequest`. We shouldn't have to remember what this `"POST"` means anymore. We just need to make a `POST` request, and how exactly that happens at the HTTP level is none of our business.

To summarize, public constants are pure evil in OOP and must not be used, ever. There can be no excuse for them. I'm aware that the modern Java, Ruby, PHP, Scala, etc. libraries are full of them, and that's unfortunate. Don't use them in *your* own code. Don't make the problem bigger. Always replace them with micro classes, no matter how small they look. Don't solve code duplication problems with public constants—use classes instead.

By the way, exactly the same must be said about `enum` in Java. These enumerations are no different than public constants and must also be avoided.

2.6 Be immutable

`Discuss at http://goo.gl/z1XGj0`

Make all classes immutable and you will do your maintainability a big favor. As everything else in this book, immutability helps us keep classes small, cohesive, decoupled from each other, and maintainable. A piece of code is easy to maintain when it is easy to understand. An immutable class is much easier to understand than a mutable one. If you make yourself think in terms of immutable objects, your code will become cleaner, shorter, and much easier to digest.

Let's discuss what *immutability* is, and then I'll show you a few practical benefits it gives to your objects.

An object is immutable if its state can't be modified after it is created. For example, an object of this class is mutable:

```
class Cash {
  private int dollars;
  public void setDollars(int val) {
    this.dollars = val;
  }
}
```

Here is a similar class, but its objects are immutable:

```
class Cash {
  private final int dollars;
  Cash(int val) {
    this.dollars = val;
  }
}
```

As you see, the difference is in the `final` keyword next to the private property `dollars`. Its presence literally tells the compiler that any attempts to modify its value outside the constructor must lead to a compile-time error. An immutable object encapsulates whatever is necessary and can't change anything later. If we need to modify an immutable object, we have to create a new one. For example, say we want to implement a little arithmetic with a simple operation of multiplication on the monetary class `Cash`. Here is a mutable example:

```
class Cash {
  private int dollars;
  public void mul(int factor) {
    this.dollars *= factor;
  }
}
```

This is how we would do the same but with an immutable class[1]:

```
class Cash {
  private final int dollars;
  public Cash mul(int factor) {
    return new Cash(this.dollars * factor);
  }
}
```

The difference is obvious. An immutable object can't modify himself in any way. He will always try to create and return another object with the new, desired characteristics.

Here is how we use a mutable object:

```
Cash five = new Cash(5);
five.mul(10);
System.out.println(five); // "$50" will be printed
```

---

[1] It's OK to use `new` operator here, even though later in the book I suggest that its usage must be limited to constructors only. Here we make an instance of the same class, not of a new dependency.

And this is how we do the same manipulation with an immutable one:

```
Cash five = new Cash(5);
Cash fifty = five.mul(10);
System.out.println(fifty); // "$50" will be printed
```

I'm getting closer to my point, which is to never make your objects mutable; always work with immutable ones. Mutable objects are an abuse of the entire object paradigm. The last two pieces of code perfectly illustrate that. Once object `five` is instantiated, it can't become `fifty`. Five is five; it will always be five until the end of its lifecycle. If we need `fifty`, we should instantiate another object. Let me show you this code again:

```
Cash five = new Cash(5);
five.mul(10);
System.out.println(five); // oops, it is "$50"
```

You see, how confusing is that last line? We are expecting our object `five` to behave like "five dollars", while it already exposes the behavior of "fifty dollars." I hope this demonstrates how mutability makes our code difficult to understand and maintain. Mutability simply makes it messy.

You may say that it's possible to name this variable `money` and solve the problem, as the code becomes clear again:

```
Cash money = new Cash(5); // it is "$5"
money.mul(10);
System.out.println(money); // it is "$50"
```

Maybe so, but only with a primitive example like this one. And only in a very limited scope. What we just did is basically replacing a more specific name with a more abstract one. In general, it's a bad tactic. In its extreme, we would name all variables as `var`. Needless to say why it's a bad idea.

Let's make it clear. I'm not saying that immutable classes are better than mutable classes, are more effective in some situations, can solve some problems more elegantly, or can be used more frequently than mutable ones. Not at all. I'm saying that mutable objects have no right to exist. Their usage must be *strictly prohibited*. They simply shouldn't be present in OOP, like what's done in Haskell, for example. All classes must instantiate immutable objects that never change their state, no matter what kind of domain it is, including gaming, UI, mobile, web, or algorithms.

There are a few well-known arguments in favor of immutability.[1] Let's go through them briefly and then discuss counterarguments that usually sound like "immutable objects are a good thing, but not for our project."

Hold on. Before we jump into those reasons, let's discuss "lazy loading", which is technically impossible to do with immutable objects. Well, at least in Java, Ruby, C++ and a few other languages I know. An object is loaded "lazily", when it updates its encapsulated properties on demand. Here is an example:

---

[1] Brian Goetz et. al., *Java Concurrency in Practice*, 1st Edition, Addison-Wesley Professional, 2006.

```
class Page {
  private final String uri;
  private String html;
  Page(String address) {
    this.uri = address;
    this.html = null;
  }
  public String content() {
    if (this.html == null) {
      this.html = /* load from network */
    }
    return this.html;
  }
}
```

This is how lazy loading works. When we construct an object, it doesn't have anything in `this.html`. There is `null` instead of real data. Then, when the first time method, `content()`, is called, we load the data from the network and store in the property. On the next call to `content()`, the roundtrip to the network is not happening. Instead, we just return what is already stored in `this.html`. Obviously, this class is mutable. Can we make it immutable? Not in Java. Do we need this lazy loading at all? Of course. Mostly for the sake of performance. We don't want to load that page multiple times, once is enough.

I think that the language itself must provide this feature. Something like this should be available:

```
@OnlyOnce
public String content() {
  return /* load from network */
}
```

This `@OnlyOnce` annotation (or something similar) should instruct the compiler that this method should only be called once

in this object. All other consecutive calls must return the value
previously returned. Unfortunately, we don't have that in Java,
at the moment of writing this. There are a number of
workarounds, where you keep the object immutable and
implement lazy loading. All of them are hacks. And all of them
are basically different caching techniques, either based on some
frameworks or static hash maps. I previously touched on this
subject in Section 1.3 and gave an example of a caching
mechanism, which may be useful, if you are not looking for a
pure immutability.

2.6.1 Identity mutability

Immutable objects don't have the problem of "identity mutability."
In a few words, this issue surfaces when we compare two objects
that look equal to each other and then later one of them changes
its state. They are no longer equal anymore, but we still think
they are. Or the other way around. In Java, for example:

```
Map<Cash, String> map = new HashMap<>();
Cash five = new Cash("$5");
Cash ten = new Cash("$10");
map.put(five, "five");
map.put(ten, "ten");
five.mul(2);
System.out.println(map); // {$10=>"five", $10=>"ten"}
```

The map is no longer correct after our manipulation. It contains
two keys that are equal to each other. How did that happen?
First, we created two objects, `five` and `ten`, that were *not*
equal to each other. Then, we put them into the map, and
`HashMap` created two entries because the keys were not equal.
Then, we modified the state of one of them, changing it from ten

to five by using the modifying method, `mul()`. The map had no idea about this manipulation. We didn't inform it in any way. We didn't give it a chance to compare all keys and remove duplicates. In the end, we have a very confusing state of the map.

Moreover, if we try to retrieve one of them, we will have an unpredictable result, since the map now is broken:

```
map.get(five); // either "ten" or "five" comes back
```

This problem is known as the "mutability of identity" and can lead to very serious and very-difficult-to-find bugs. Indeed, look again at the code above. If I remove all lines before the last one, would you be able to guess why `map.toString()` returns such a strange state? Would you be able to easily understand why and how `HashMap` contains duplicate keys? And this is just an example with five lines of code.

This would not happen with an immutable object, because after it gets into the map, we won't be able to modify its state. The `HashMap` will calculate its hash code based on the state, place it into an internal hash table, and keep it there. The only way to do anything with the entry in the map is to add a new key object to it. Immutable objects completely eliminate problems related to identity mutability.

2.6.2 Failure atomicity

Another advantage of immutable objects is their "failure atomicity", which means that we either have a complete and solid object or a failure[1]—nothing in between. Consider this example of the mutable class `Cash`:

---

[1] Joshua Bloch, *Effective Java*, 2nd Edition, Addison-Wesley, 2008.

```
class Cash {
  private int dollars;
  private int cents;
  public void mul(int factor) {
    this.dollars *= factor;
    if (/* something is wrong */) {
      throw new RuntimeException("oops...");
    }
    this.cents *= factor;
  }
}
```

If I call method `mul()` and it throws an exception, half of the object will be modified (`this.dollars`), and the other half will be left intact (`this.cents`). This may lead to very serious and, again, very difficult-to-find bugs. Immutable objects don't have this flaw, because they never modify anything inside them. Instead, they instantiate new objects with a new state:

```
class Cash {
  private final int dollars;
  private final int cents;
  public Cash mul(int factor) {
    if (/* something is wrong */) {
      throw new RuntimeException("oops...");
    }
    return new Cash(
      this.dollars * factor,
      this.cents * factor
    );
  }
}
```

Obviously, it is possible to achieve this "failure atomicity" with mutable objects too, but we would have to pay special attention to do this. With immutable objects, on the other hand, we get this atomicity out of the box—there's no need to worry about it, as all objects are "atomic" by definition. What is wrong about ensuring failure atomicity explicitly in a mutable object? The complexity of the object will be much higher and, because of that, the likelihood of a mistake is bigger. And, of course, the maintainability of such an object will be seriously affected. For example, here is how a mutable and failure atomicity savvy `Cash` class would look:

```
class Cash {
  private int dollars;
  private int cents;
  public void mul(int factor) {
    int before = this.dollars;
    this.dollars *= factor;
    if (/* something is wrong with cents */) {
      this.dollars = before;
      throw new RuntimeException("oops...");
    }
    this.cents *= factor;
  }
}
```

We're saving `this.dollars` to a temporary variable, in order to have an ability to restore its value, right before we throw an exception. With such a small object it is not a big deal, but when it starts to grow in size, we can easily miss the property we have to restore. And even in this small object, the code is rather messy, isn't it?

By the way, I'm listing the advantages of immutable objects in order of importance, as I understand them—from the least to the most. So, the most important advantages are still ahead.

2.6.3 Temporal coupling

The next benefit you get from using immutable objects is the lack of "temporal coupling." The best way to explain this is by example:

```
Cash price = new Cash();
price.setDollars(29);
price.setCents(95);
System.out.println(price); // "$29.95"
```

This is a very simple example, but it's how mutable objects are usually instantiated *and* initialized. First, we create a "skeleton" that has `NULL`-s for all private properties (instantiation). Then, we "set" them using "setters" (initialization). This is how JavaBeans, JPA, JAXB, and other standards recommend you work with objects in Java. You probably already understand that I'm not a big fan of all of these standards, to say the least. They are well-designed instruments for procedural programmers using Java syntax, but they are absolutely wrong in terms of true "object thinking." This `Cash` class is a perfect Java "bean", which is a bag of data and a few procedures attached to it. First, we create a bag, then we inject data into it, and then we instruct it to manipulate the data for us. Try to stay away from these "standards" as much as possible...

There are four lines of Java code in the example above. They go one after another in a very specific order. They are coupled to each other in chronological order. If I, by mistake, reorder them like this, the logic will be broken, but the code will still compile:

```
Cash price = new Cash();
price.setDollars(29);
System.out.println(price); // "$29.00"!
price.setCents(95);
```

It's a very simple example, and you might say there is absolutely no motivation for this reordering. I shouldn't do it, and that's it. Yes, that may be true in this particular example, because I can understand the logic of the code in a few seconds. But still, I have to *understand* the temporal coupling between lines before I can modify them. The compiler won't help me. Reordering the lines is technically still a valid operation. In other words, it is my problem to remember which line goes first and which one goes next. And guess what, it's a big *maintainability* issue if there are many mutable objects and I need to remember their order or what manipulation I performed with them. How about this code, for example:

```
Cash price = new Cash();
// 50 lines of code to calculate X
price.setDollars(x);
// 30 more lines to calculate Y
price.setCents(y);
// 25 lines here to do something else
System.out.println(price);
```

Will it be easy to understand that this particular order of "setters" has to be preserved and they all should occur before the `println()`? Absolutely not. Here is how this problem is solved by immutability:

```
Cash price = new Cash(29, 95);
System.out.println(price); // "$29.95"
```

The object is instantiated in one statement—always. We simply can't separate *instantiation* from *initialization*. They always remain together. I can't change the order of these two lines, because then the code won't compile. Thus, immutability entirely removes any temporal coupling between statements in code. Before I can do anything with an object, I have to fully initialize it. Then it doesn't matter what happens. The object is self-sufficient and solid. No more initialization is required.

2.6.4 Side effect-free

When an object is mutable, basically anyone can modify it on the fly. Let's say I'm passing a `price` object to the method that is supposed to print it. However, there is a mistake in the method. Besides printing the price, it multiplies it by two:

```
void print(Cash price) {
  System.out.println(
    "Today price is: " + price
  );
  price.mul(2);
  System.out.println(
    "Buy now, tomorrow price is: " + price
  );
}
```

Now when I call this method, I experience a "side effect":

```
Cash five = new Cash(5);
print(five);
System.out.println(five); // "$10", oops...
```

It will take some time to find out what's going on. I will have to debug every single manipulation with `five` in order to spot the place where that mistake is happening. With this simple code, debugging may only take a few minutes, but with a couple thousand lines of code and a few hundred classes, I may spend several days.

On the other hand, if my class `Cash` is immutable, nobody is able to modify it anywhere. And I'm sure about this. I won't search my code for side effects if something doesn't work. The immutability of `Cash` will make me confident that `five` always means "five dollars" at any moment in time and in any place.

2.6.5 No NULL references

We'll discuss why `NULL` is pure evil in OOP in Sections 4.1 and 3.3, but here it's about "unset" object properties. For example:

```
class User {
  private final int id;
  private String name = null;
  public User(int num) {
    this.id = num;
  }
  public void setName(String txt) {
    this.name = txt;
  }
}
```

When an instance of this class is made, the property `name` is set to `NULL`. It will be initialized later in `setName()` if it is ever called. Until then, it's `NULL`. What's wrong with that, you may ask? Just check for `NULL` before touching it and you'll be safe, right? Yes, true, but the code will be polluted by those "`if name != null`" checks. And if we forget to check, we'll have a `NullPointerException` or a "segmentation fault" in C++. But these are not the main problems. After all, `NULL` is not very different from, say, an empty string. We may check for it from time to time, and there is nothing wrong with it. It happens.

The main problem is bigger. And it's about ... you guessed it ... *maintainability*. An object that may have `NULL` instead of real properties is way less maintainable, mostly because it's difficult to understand when it is still the object and when it has morphed into something that's *not an object*. Let me explain what that means by asking a question first: Why might we need to have an object of class `User` without a name being initialized? Seriously, when and why might we have such a necessity?

I think I know the answer. In most cases, this happens when we need *another* class, but we are too lazy to create it. Or we just don't know how to create it. Or we don't understand what a class is in OOP. There could be many reasons, but the result is the same: a very big class, which is a user, a customer, an employee, and a database record at the same time. When `name` is initialized, it is a customer. When it's `NULL`, it is a user, etc.

We simply don't know how to use inheritance and encapsulation in order to break the problem down into pieces. That's why we use the same class when a new requirement comes in. But in order to somehow manage its diverse behavior, we have to use these "temporarily unset" properties. By their initialization status (`NULL` or not), we understand who our object is—a user, a customer, or an SQL record. Needless to say, that is a terrible practice.

The very existence of `NULL` encourages us to follow this bad practice. However, if you make all objects immutable, you won't be able to have any `NULL`-s inside them. In other words, you will be *forced* to create small, solid, and cohesive objects—much more maintainable objects.

2.6.6 Thread safety

Thread safety is a quality of an object that literally means that the object can be used concurrently from a few threads, and its results will still be *predictable*. Here is an example of a class that instantiates objects that aren't thread-safe:

```
class Cash {
  private int dollars;
  private int cents;
  public void mul(int factor) {
    this.dollars *= factor;
    this.cents *= factor;
  }
}
```

It looks innocent, but let's see what will happen if I run this code in two parallel threads:

```
Cash price = new Cash("$15.10");
// the next two lines in two threads
price.mul(2);
// "$30.20" and "$60.40" expected
System.out.println(price);
```

Try it yourself and you will see that on every run, a different number is printed. There are only two valid results expected. The first thread prints `$30.20`, and the second one prints `$60.40`, which means the first thread was multiplied by two and the second one multiplied it again. However, you will sometimes see `$60.20`. Why is that happening and what does this number really mean? How is it possible to multiply `$15.10` by two and obtain `$60.20`?

That's easy. One thread multiplies dollars by two and cents by two while another thread, at the same time, multiplies dollars again, but doesn't manage to multiply cents yet because it runs out of time. It will multiply later, of course, but for a few microseconds our object `price` is in a "broken" state—dollars have already been multiplied while cents haven't yet.

This is one of the hardest problems to find, debug, and resolve, mostly because it's very difficult (and sometimes impossible) to reproduce. You need to run the test multiple times, and there is no guarantee that the problem will surface.

Immutable objects completely resolve this problem by disabling any modifications to their state in runtime. No matter how many threads are working with the object at the same time, none of them can modify its state.

You can also make a mutable class thread-safe by using explicit synchronization:

```
class Cash {
  private int dollars;
  private int cents;
  public void mul(int factor) {
    synchronized (this) {
      this.dollars *= factor;
      this.cents *= factor;
    }
  }
}
```

This will work, but there are a few issues with the approach. First, it's not so easy to add thread safety to a mutable class. Second, adding synchronization always comes at a cost to performance. Now, each thread has to wait for an object to be released in order to start working with it. Each thread will *exclusively lock* the object, and all other threads will sit and wait.

Also, don't forget about possible deadlocks. That is very dark territory. I strongly recommend that you stay away from it and use immutable objects.

By the way, this is the code to experiment with the `Cash` class above:

```java
class Cash {
  private int dollars;
  private int cents;
  Cash(final int dlr, final int cts) {
    this.dollars = dlr;
    this.cents = cts;
  }
  @Override
  public String toString() {
    return String.format(
      "$%d.%d", this.dollars, this.cents
    );
  }
  public void mul(int factor) {
    this.dollars *= factor;
    this.cents *= factor;
  }
}
final Cash cash = new Cash(15, 10);
final CountDownLatch start = new CountDownLatch(1);
final Callable<Object> script = new Callable<>() {
  @Override
  public Object call() throws Exception {
    start.await(); // here
    cash.mul(2);
    System.out.println(cash);
    return null;
  }
};
final ExecutorService svc =
  Executors.newCachedThreadPool();
svc.submit(script); // first thread
svc.submit(script); // second thread
start.countDown();
```

Run it a few times in your IDE and check the output. To make it even more interesting, add a few more `svc.submit(script)` lines to it.

Of course, the script must `shutdown()` the `svc` at the end. I skipped that part for the sake of brevity.

2.6.7 Smaller and simpler objects

And now, my favorite benefit of immutability: *simplicity*. And as you already understand, simplicity translates into maintainability. The simpler the objects, the more cohesive and maintainable they are. The more complex the software, the lower the quality of the programmer who created it. The best software is simple—it is easy to understand, modify, document, support, and refactor. Maintainability is the most important virtue of modern programming.

In most cases, simplicity merely means fewer lines of code. The shorter the class, the easier it is to understand what it does, where it fails, and how to refactor it. When there are 1,000 lines of code in a class, it is obvious that even its author has no idea what the class is doing. In Java, I would say the maximum size of a class is *250 lines of code*, including comments and empty lines. Anything above this number is a flashing signal of the need for refactoring. In Ruby, I would suggest you stay under 100 lines.

It doesn't really matter what the exact number is, as longer as it is "small." I've seen classes with 5,000 lines of code. That is absolutely unacceptable, and there is no excuse for that. By the way, I've even seen them in OpenJDK sources. Don't even want to mention Android SDK.

If you can keep the lengths of all classes in an entire application under the 250-line limit, I would say you are a good software developer and an architect. If you can get even lower, you are awesome. I'm talking about both production and test code.

Immutable objects are naturally smaller than mutable ones, simply because it's very difficult to make an immutable object too big—it initializes the state only in the ctor. You won't make a ctor with 10 arguments; it will look extremely ugly, and you will notice this ugliness all along the way. You start with a small object that has a few arguments in the ctor. Then you start to add new features to it, and as the object grows, so does its ctor. Every time you add a new "feature" to it, you will have to make its ctor bigger. Very soon, you will realize that something has gone wrong and will break the class down into smaller classes. You will never reach 2,000 lines with an immutable class.

I think this argument is the strongest. Immutability makes classes cleaner and shorter. That's the most important advantage you get by making your classes immutable.

At the beginning of this section, I promised to discuss arguments against immutability, but I won't do it here. I'll do it later in Section 3.4, simply because the answer to all these arguments is one and the same. Stay with me for a few more sections, and we'll get to the criticism of immutability and my position on it.

To summarize this section, let me repeat what I said in Section 2.6: I'm strongly against mutable objects. In true object-oriented software, only immutable objects may exist. Mutability is a terrible inheritance of procedural programming. Never make any classes mutable. Period.

2.7 Write tests instead of documentation

Documentation is a very important component of maintainability. Well, not the documentation specifically, but the accessibility of additional information about the class or the method in question. As a reader of your code, I may need additional details or simply some extra explanation. I may not be as smart as you are. I may not know how your sorting algorithm works, what MD5 is, how this particular regular expression works, or what the purpose of `/dev/null` is. That is all very possible. In my experience, it's very annoying to read through code written by a "know it all."

To make your code easier for me to read, *assume* I'm a junior programmer who has very little understanding about the business domain, the programming language, design patterns, and algorithms. Assume I'm much dumber than yourself. This is how you will show me your respect—not by showing off and demonstrating your skills, but by writing simple, easy-to-read code. Bad programmers write complex code. Good programmers write simple code.

Ideal code explains itself and doesn't need any additional documentation. For example:

```
Employee jeff = department.employee("Jeff");
jeff.giveRaise(new Cash("$5,000"));
if (jeff.performance() < 3.5) {
  jeff.fire();
}
```

Do we need to document this code any more? I think it's clear as is. What about this one:

```
class Helper {
  int saveAndCheck(float x) { .. }
  float extract(String text) { .. }
  boolean convert(int value, boolean extra) { .. }
}
```

It's a terrible class name (Section 1.1) with terrible names for methods (Section 2.4), and the entire design of the "class" is terrible. Obviously, it needs documentation. I simply can't understand what it does, what these methods are for, or how to use them. Bad design forces me to write documentation. This means that good and maintainable classes don't need documentation. Their purpose is clear, and their design is compact and elegant. For example:

```
class WebPage {
  String content() { .. }
  void update(String content) { .. }
}
```

Thus, I would say don't document your code; make it clean instead.

And by "making it clean", I mean also creating unit tests. Even though unit testing has only just appeared as a common practice,[1] a unit test must be treated as a part of a class, just like its methods, properties, name, and a list of interfaces. Unfortunately, this is not how it's done in most languages (or maybe *all*?). In Java, for example, a unit test is a `.java` file with another class inside it. If we have a class `Cash`, then our test "class" will be named `CashTest`, by convention. That's not an ideal approach, mostly because it allows us to create classes without unit tests. That should not happen.

---

[1] Kent Beck, *Test-Driven Development by Example*, Addison Wesley, 2003.

A unit test is *part* of a class, not a standalone entity. I mean, conceptually, not technically. Technically, in all languages I know, a unit test is a separate file.

By creating a clean and maintainable unit test, you are making the class cleaner and more maintainable. That's why the better the unit test is, the less documentation is required. A unit test *is* the documentation. A unit test, if written properly, will greatly help me understand your class. And it's international. I don't need to be fluent in English to understand a unit test in Java, but in order to understand Javadoc text, I need some English reading skills.

Just as they say a picture is worth a thousand words, I would say a unit test is worth a page of documentation. A unit test *demonstrates* to me how to use the class, while documentation tells a story that is much more difficult to understand and interpret. Don't tell, demonstrate. And try to make your demonstrations entertaining enough. If you manage to make them right, they will be read much more often than the code of the class itself.

The best recommendation I can give for writing good, clean unit tests would be to treat them with the exact same attention as your "main" code. There are many other good tips for unit testing in general and quality of tests in particular in *Working Effectively With Legacy Code*[1] and *Clean Code.*[2]

A few reviewers asked me to provide an example of a good unit test here. I will do it mostly to illustrate this chapter with some

---

[1] Michael Feathers, *Working Effectively With Legacy Code*, Prentice Hall, 2004.
[2] Robert C. Martin, *Clean Code: A Handbook of Agile Software Craftsmanship*, Prentice Hall, 2008.

code. The problem of writing good unit tests is definitely outside the scope of this book. Here is what I would call a good test for class `Cash` (using JUnit and Hamcrest):

```
class CashTest {
  @Test
  public void summarizes() {
    assertThat(
      new Cash("$5").plus(new Cash("$3")),
      equalTo(new Cash("$8"))
    )
  }
  @Test
  public void deducts() {
    assertThat(
      new Cash("$7").plus(new Cash("-$11")),
      equalTo(new Cash("-$4"))
    )
  }
  @Test
  public void multiplies() {
    assertThat(
      new Cash("$2").mul(3),
      equalTo(new Cash("$6"))
    )
  }
}
```

You will find a lot of good advice on how to write unit tests in *Growing Object-Oriented Software, Guided by Tests*.[1]

---

[1] Steve Freeman et al., *Growing Object-Oriented Software, Guided by Tests*, Addison-Wesley Professional, 2009

2.8 Don't mock; use fakes

Discuss at http://goo.gl/OF3Cev

One more section about unit testing, and then we are done with them. This time it is about *mocking* as an instrument for optimizing tests. This is how it works, in a nutshell. Let's say we have a class `Cash` that can convert itself to a new currency:

```
class Cash {
  private final Exchange exchange;
  private final int cents;
  public Cash(Exchange exch, int cnts) {
    this.exchange = exch;
    this.cents = cnts;
  }
  public Cash in(String currency) {
    return new Cash(
      this.exchange,
      this.cents * this.exchange.rate(
        "USD", currency
      )
    );
  }
}
```

The class depends on some `Exchange` that actually knows the rate of conversion for USD to, say, EUR. To use class `Cash`, we have to provide an instance of `Exchange` to its constructor:

```
Cash dollar = new Cash(new NYSE("secret"), 100);
Cash euro = dollar.in("EUR");
```

Here, class `NYSE` knows how to find that USD-to-EUR exchange rate at the New York Stock Exchange, probably by making an HTTP request to its server. I'm using the `"secret"` string here as a password for the production server at `NYSE`. This is how `Cash` works in production, but we don't want to make that request to a live `NYSE` server on every run of our unit tests. We also don't want to disclose this `"secret"` to all programmers. We need to find a way to test `Cash` without involving `NYSE`.

A traditional approach is called "mocking." Instead of using `NYSE`, we create a "mock" of interface `Exchange` and use it as an argument of the `Cash` ctor (I'm using Mockito[1]):

```
Exchange exchange = Mockito.mock(Exchange.class);
Mockito.doReturn(1.15)
   .when(exchange)
   .rate("USD", "EUR")
Cash dollar = new Cash(exchange, 500);
Cash euro = dollar.in("EUR");
assert "5.75".equals(euro.toString());
```

I'm sure you are aware of this technique. I just decided to explain it so that it's easier for us to now discuss why I think it's a bad practice. Yes, I'm saying that mocking is a bad practice and should be used as a last resort. Well, if you design all your objects as this book recommends, you won't have any need for mocking.

Instead of mocking, I suggest you use "fake" objects. Here is how interface `Exchange` should be shipped to its users:

---

[1]To my knowledge, it's here: `http://mockito.org/`

```
interface Exchange {
  float rate(String origin, String target);
  final class Fake implements Exchange {
    @Override
    float rate(String origin, String target) {
      return 1.2345;
    }
  }
}
```

This nested "fake" class is part of the interface and is shipped together with the interface. It is a valuable part of `Exchange`, because it helps everybody use `Exchange` in unit tests. That's not all, but more about it later. Now, have a look at a unit test that uses a "fake" class instead of mocking:

```
Exchange exchange = new Exchange.Fake();
Cash dollar = new Cash(exchange, 500);
Cash euro = dollar.in("EUR");
assert "6.17".equals(euro.toString());
```

It looks shorter, doesn't it? You might say it's not so obvious now—Where does this `6.17` come from if we don't specify the rate anywhere? That's true. But we can make our "fake" class even more powerful. We can make it smart enough that it returns an encapsulated rate instead of a constant one. In general, "fake" classes can and should be rather powerful. I would even say that sometimes, they will be more complex than "real" classes. Also, they may implement that required functionality in a rather different way than production classes. They may act and respond differently. It's not a big problem, as long as your unit tests don't rely too much on their specific behavior. Don't write your tests to satisfy "fake" classes. Instead, make sure your "fake" classes are serving your tests properly.

"Fake" classes make tests shorter, which seriously improves their maintainability. Mocking, on the other hand, makes tests very verbose and very difficult to understand and refactor. With a simple interface `Exchange`, this may not be so obvious, but we already managed to save one line in the test. When the test involves five objects from different classes, each having a few methods, this wireframing of Mockito calls will look totally cryptic to anyone in a few months—even for the author of the test.

But it's not just about verbosity. The problem is much bigger. Mocking makes unit tests hard to maintain because it *turns assumptions into facts*. Let me explain what I mean. Look at these two lines again:

```
Exchange exchange = Mockito.mock(Exchange.class);
Mockito.doReturn(1.15)
  .when(exchange)
  .rate("USD", "EUR");
```

What exactly are we saying here? We literally say, "we assume that `Cash` calls `Exchange.rate()`." Our entire unit test is built on this assumption. We don't know this for sure, because in the unit test, class `Cash` is a "black box" for us. We don't know how exactly the method `Cash.in()` is implemented and how exactly it uses an instance of `Exchange`. Maybe it doesn't use it at all. We don't know, but we are making an *assumption* and building the entire test around it. We are turning this assumption into a fact. We are saying, "this is how we know `Cash` works!"

That's bad. It's very bad. Why? Because it goes against the entire purpose of unit testing—to be a safety net for refactoring.

A unit test helps me refactor a class because it fails when I do something that changes the behavior of the class (true positive).

But at the same time, it doesn't fail if I don't change the behavior (false positive). That's a very important "second half" of the entire idea—it must *not fail* if I don't make any changes to the class' public behavior. It must not give me false positive indicators.

However, our unit test will fail for no reason. Here is how. Let's say we modify the interface `Exchange`, and now it looks like this:

```
interface Exchange {
  float rate(String target);
  float rate(String origin, String target);
}
```

The first method (with one argument) returns the USD-to-target rate, while the second method (with two arguments) allows us to specify both origin and target currencies.

Then, we make our class `Cash` use this new method, with one argument, when the origin currency is USD. What will happen with our unit test? That's right, it will fail. It will give me a false indicator of a failure while there is no failure. Class `Cash` still works fine and converts currencies. Everything is still perfectly valid, but the test fails.

This is very annoying and completely ruins my trust in my own unit tests. That's one of the key reasons why so many programmers don't like unit tests and don't use them. They are too fragile and unstable—mostly due to mocking. Let's see what happens in the exact same situation, but with "fake" class `Exchange.Fake` instead of mocking.

When we change interface `Exchange`, we automatically change the implementation of class `Exchange.Fake`, and it looks like this now:

```
interface Exchange {
  float rate(String target);
  float rate(String origin, String target);
  final class Fake implements Exchange {
    @Override
    float rate(String target) {
      return this.rate("USD", target);
    }
    @Override
    float rate(String origin, String target) {
      return 1.2345;
    }
  }
}
```

Do we need to change the unit test? No. Does it break? No. We didn't change the behavior of `Cash`, and the unit test didn't give us any false signals. It's a good unit test, and I can trust it.

The point is that mocking is a *bad practice* in the first place. It was invented in order to help us with unit testing, but it doesn't do us a favor. It couples our tests to internal details of the class implementation. We make assumptions, hard-code them in mocks, and call it a day. When the time for refactoring comes, we can only throw our tests away, because they are coupled with an implementation that is no longer valid.

To the contrary, "fake" classes make tests fully maintainable, because we don't care how our class `Cash` communicates with `Exchange`. This interaction between two classes is not any of our concern in the unit test of class `Cash`. It's the private business of `Cash`. Maybe he will communicate with `Exchange`, maybe not. Maybe he will use a one-argument method, or maybe a two-argument one. It's up to class `Cash`. We have no right to assume anything about its internal decisions. The only thing we care about is how `Cash` interacts with us, not how he interacts with someone else.

You might say that we give an instance of `Exchange` to the object of class `Cash`, so we have the right to know how he uses it. No, we don't. We don't have the right to know *how* the object is implemented. Making our tests aware of internal implementation details of an object makes the test fragile and unmaintainable. The root of this problem is mocking.

Again, mocking is a terrible practice.

Moreover, most mocking frameworks give us the ability to verify whether certain interactions happened with the mocked object and how many times. This may look convenient, but it's a very bad idea, for the same reason. By making unit tests dependable on interactions, we make refactoring painful and sometimes impossible. We must not check or test how the object works with its dependencies. This is the information for the object to encapsulate. In other words, to hide from us. It's a secret.

But what can we do if there is no "fake" shipped with an interface? Of course it would be perfect to have "fake" classes everywhere, attached to all interfaces, but in reality that's not the case, right? Yes, right. The reality, in general, is much less elegant than the practices described in this book. However, we can change it—the reality, not the book. Start with your own interfaces and equip them with "fake" classes. Make sure every class you create doesn't have interface-less methods (see Section 2.3) and provide "fake" classes for all interfaces. That's how you start changing the world. Users of your classes will start writing better tests, and the amount of mocking in this world will start to decrease.

There is also an important advantage of "fake" classes that I promised to describe above: they help you better think through the design of the interface. When working with an interface and creating a "fake" class for it, you inevitably have to think like a user of your interface, not only its author. Look at it from a different angle, and try to implement the same functionality by using "test" resources.

Take, for example, the interface `WebPage`. Its default implementation would be to make an HTTP GET request in order to load the page content, and another PUT request to update the content. But how would you implement a "fake" class for it? Where would this content be stored? How do you make sure these read and update operations are thread-safe? How do you deal with different encodings? There will be many questions. The point is that by answering them and finding the optimal solution, you will inevitably improve the interface.

Thus, stay away from mocking, and always create "fake" classes for your interfaces.

I can also give you a few practical examples of really big fake classes we use in our projects. Not just classes, but packages of classes and packages of packages. For example, in one case, we were writing a RESTful client of GitHub API. The API itself is rather big, has over 150 entry points. In order to unit test the client, we created a full copy of the API with fake classes. In order to preserve the data and fully imitate GitHub, we were using an XML file. Over 150 fake classes were updating that big XML storage and the client didn't have a clue that it was talking to a fake GitHub, not a real server. The implementation of this fake library took some time, but that was a valuable investment, since unit testing became very simple and compact[1].

In another example, we had a persistence layer in AWS DynamoDB and a collection of interfaces in the "model." Then, we had classes that implemented that interfaces, by making real interactions with that hosted NoSQL database. On top of that, for testing purposes, we nested a fake class in each interface, which were emulating persistence by using plain files. This collection of fake classes made our tests much shorter and cleaner[2].

---

[1] http://github.com/jcabi/jcabi-github
[2] http://github.com/yegor256/rultor

2.9 Keep interfaces short; use smarts

Discuss at http://goo.gl/1Zos9r

I've mentioned already in Section 1.2, that a properly designed, solid, and cohesive class would have just a few public methods. We'll discuss that in even more detail in Section 3.1, but I'm sure you already understand the importance of keeping classes small. It is even more important to make interfaces small. Why more important? Because a class might implement a number of interfaces. If two interfaces have five methods each, a class implementing both of them will have to have 10 public methods. That would not be an elegant class.

Remember the interface `Exchange` from the previous section? This one:

```
interface Exchange {
  float rate(String target);
  float rate(String source, String target);
}
```

It was good enough for the purpose of discussion in that section, but it's a terrible design, because it *demands* too much. An interface is a contract that an implementing class must obey. This interface puts too many demands on its implementer. Such a contract encourages us to violate the well-known Single Responsibility Principle, or in other words, create non-cohesive classes. This contract demands an exchange to calculate a rate *and* apply a default currency when it's not provided. These are two separate functions, even though they stay very close to each other. I'm saying that the one-argument method `rate()` should not be in this interface.

Should we define another interface for it? No. We should create a "smart" class, right inside the interface:

```
interface Exchange {
  float rate(String source, String target);
  final class Smart {
    private final Exchange origin;
    public float toUsd(String source) {
      return this.origin.rate(source, "USD");
    }
  }
}
```

There can be many more methods in this "smart" class that do something very obvious and very common. This "smart" class doesn't know how an exchange is implemented and how that rate is calculated, but it applies a certain functionality on top of it. This functionality can be shared between different implementations of `Exchange`.

So, this is another reason for making these "smarts" and shipping them together with interfaces—we don't want different interface implementations to re-write the same functionality again and again. Fetching the rate from the New York Stock Exchange is a unique feature of the `NYSE` class, which implements `Exchange`. But applying the `"USD"` currency to the call when it's not provided is a function we can easily share.

This is how the `Exchange.Smart` nested class would be used in combination with `NYSE`:

```
float rate = new Exchange.Smart(new NYSE())
  .toUsd("EUR");
```

Let's say we want to add more functionality to the `NYSE` and, at the same time, to all other implementations of `Exchange`. Let's say we need to convert from USD to EUR very often and we want to avoid code duplication. We don't want to use this `"EUR"` string literal everywhere. We just need something like the `eurToUsd()` method. We don't add it to the `Exchange` interface. Instead, we put into the "smart" class. Now it has two methods:

```
interface Exchange {
  float rate(String source, String target);
  final class Smart {
    private final Exchange origin;
    public float toUsd(String source) {
      return this.origin.rate(source, "USD");
    }
    public float eurToUsd() {
      return this.toUsd("EUR");
    }
  }
}
```

Now, we can get this EUR to USD rate with this one call:

```
float rate = new Exchange.Smart(new NYSE())
  .eurToUsd();
```

The "smart" class is growing in size, while the `Exchange` interface stays small and cohesive. It contains just one method, which is implemented by `NYSE`, `XE`, `Yahoo`, and any other currency rate providers. The functionality we add in this "smart" class is not specific to the exchange. It is shared among all exchanges. There is no need to demand its implementation from each exchange. No need to make interface `Exchange` too demanding.

That's why the title and the subject of this section: keep interfaces short. Interfaces are contracts between us, users of the exchange, and implementers of class `NYSE`. The longer the interface, the more demanding it is and the more problematic it will be for the `NYSE` author to implement. And it's not just about more work. It's about a serious loss of cohesiveness and robustness of the class. The `NYSE` class is supposed to do some over-the-network calls to the New York Stock Exchange and that's it. All other features, like knowing about EUR and converting to it, is something someone else can do. That someone else (the "smart" class) must not know anything the over-the-network calls. We basically extract shared functionality and avoid code duplication by making interfaces short and shipping "smart" classes together with them.

This approach is very close to composable decorators we're going to discuss in Section 3.2.6. The difference between a decorator and a "smart" class is that the "smart" class is increasing the amount of methods of an object, while a decorator makes existing methods more powerful. Consider this example:

```
interface Exchange {
  float rate(String origin, String target);
  final class Fast implements Exchange {
    private final Exchange origin;
    @Override
    public float rate(String source, String target) {
      final float rate;
      if (source.equals(target)) {
        rate = 1.0f;
      } else {
        rate = this.origin.rate(source, target);
      }
      return rate;
    }
    public float toUsd(String source) {
      return this.origin.rate(source, "USD");
    }
  }
}
```

This nested class, `Exchange.Fast`, is at the same time a decorator and a "smart" class. First, it overrides method `rate()`, making it more powerful. It will skip the roundtrip to the exchange if both currencies are the same. Second, it adds a new method, `toUsd()`, which makes conversion to USD more convenient.

Chapter 3

Employment

The main difference between OOP and its procedural ancestor is who is in charge. In procedural programming, the code with statements, operators, and instructions is king. The instructions control the data, manipulate them, modify them, and read them. The data is a passive component that sits tight, waiting for the code to visit and modify it somehow. Sub-routines and data structures are two basic instruments for decomposition of a bigger problem into smaller ones.

Object-oriented programming turns all this upside down. In OOP, the object is king, which is a smart replacement for the data. Instructions, statements, and operators are not in charge anymore. Actually, in a pure and perfect object-oriented language, they should not exist at all. There should be no operators, only classes and their instances. In OOP, we compose smaller objects into a bigger one, the size of an entire application, and let it do its job.

I realize that all of this may sound very abstract and theoretical, but I want to assure you that it is indeed very practical. In the next few sections, I'll explain and show you some examples. In a few words, this chapter argues against big objects, static methods, `NULL` references, getters, setters, and the `new` operator.

3.1 Expose fewer than five public methods

A *small* object is the most elegant, maintainable, cohesive, and testable kind of object. I already suggested in Subsection 2.6.7 that you keep all classes under 250 lines of code, but that's not the most important metric. We can have a class with 50 lines and 20 methods. Is that a small class? Not really. How about another example: a class with one public method and 20 private methods. Is that a small class? I would not call it a big one.

So, I'm suggesting you use the number of public (and protected) methods as a primary metric of class size. The more public methods, the bigger the class. The bigger the class, the lower its maintainability. The number I have in mind is *five*. If there are fewer than five public methods in a class, that's acceptable. If there are more, the class needs refactoring. Something is wrong with it.

Pay attention that I'm talking about public methods, not constructors and not private methods. Protected methods also fall under this category.

So why five? There's no particular reason; it's just how I feel. Can we really find out the "right" number? I don't think so. Do you have to take this number five as an absolute and mandatory constraint? No. This number is going to help you understand that there is a limit and it's very small. It's not 10, it's not 20, and it's not even seven. It is very small. Create a few methods and you're close to five. Stop and think. Are you still working with a solid and cohesive class responsible for one thing? Maybe it's time to break it down into pieces. I want you to stop and think somewhere after the fourth method and before the fifth.

So what do we get from making classes small? The answer is elegance, maintainability, cohesiveness, and testability.

Smaller classes are more *elegant* simply because they give us fewer opportunities to make a mistake. It's easier to keep three methods "in harmony" than 10 methods. They will match better.

Smaller classes are more *maintainable* because... they are smaller. There's less code, there are fewer methods, it's easier to find an error, and it's easier to modify. It's easier to isolate a problem when there are only a few entry points to an object, and each method is an entry point.

Smaller classes are more *cohesive*, meaning that their methods and properties stay "closer" to each other. In simple terms, each method uses all properties—this is what cohesiveness is about. If one property is only used in two methods and another one is used in three other methods, we can easily say that this class has two parts that are barely related to each other. The cohesiveness of such a class is low. When a class is small, the chances are higher that all its methods will interact with all properties.

Smaller classes are more *testable*, because it's easier to reproduce all their usage scenarios. Well, there aren't very many scenarios, that's why. If a class has just one public method, we can easily write all important tests for it. When there are 10 methods, the test will either be huge or we'll never create it.

I have nothing else to say here. Count your methods and keep the number under five. That's it.

3.2 Don't use static methods

Discuss at http://goo.gl/8ql2ov

Static methods, huh... This is one of my favorite subjects. It took me a few years to realize how important this problem is, and now I regret all that time I spent writing procedural software instead of object-oriented. I was blind, but now I see. Static methods are as big a mistake in OOP languages as `NULL`, or maybe even bigger. Static methods should never have been present in Java and all the other OOP languages in the first place, but they are there. We shouldn't have to know about such things as `static` keywords in Java, but alas, we have them. I don't know who exactly authored them in OOP, but they are pure evil. The static methods, not the authors. I hope.

Let's look at what they are and why we keep making them. Let's say that I need the functionality of a web page loaded through HTTP requests. So I create this "class":

```
class WebPage {
  public static String read(String uri) {
    // make HTTP request and convert
    // the response into a UTF-8 string
  }
}
```

Then, I use it in a very convenient way:

```
String html = WebPage.read("http://www.java.com");
```

This method, `read()`, is exactly the kind of static method I'm strongly against. I suggest you use objects instead (I also changed the name of the method, as Section 2.4 recommends):

```
class WebPage {
  private final String uri;
  public String content() {
    // make HTTP request and convert
    // the response into a UTF-8 string
  }
}
```

Here is how we use it:

```
String html = new WebPage("http://www.java.com")
  .content();
```

There's not a big difference, you might say. Static is even faster, because it doesn't make us create a new object every time we just want to read the content of a web page. Just call a static method, do the job, get the result, and move on. There's no need to bother with an object and then with its garbage collection. Besides, we can group many static methods into a "utility" class and call it, say, `WebUtils`. They will help us read web pages, update them, get statistical information, calculate response time, etc. There will be many methods, and they will be very easy and convenient to use. Moreover, static methods are very intuitive to use. Everybody understands how they work. Just say `WebPage.read()` and you get the idea—the page will be read. We give the computer an instruction, and it executes it. Simple and clear, right? Absolutely wrong!

The use of static methods, in any context, is a perfect indicator of a bad programmer who has no idea what OOP is. There can be no excuse for a static method in any situation. And performance concerns don't count either. Static methods are an abuse of the object paradigm. They happen to exist in Java, Ruby, C++, PHP, and others. Unfortunately. We can't get them out of there, and we can't rewrite all the open-source libraries that are full of them, but we can stop using them in our code.

We have to stop using static methods.

Now let's look at them from a few different angles and discuss practical disadvantages. I can summarize them all in advance for you: static methods make software less maintainable. That shouldn't be a surprise to you. It's all about maintainability.

3.2.1 Object vs. computer thinking

I originally labeled this section as "object vs. procedural thinking", but then renamed it. "Procedural" is almost the same, but "thinking like a computer" better describes the problem. We have inherited this type of thinking from earlier programming languages, like Assembly, C, COBOL, Basic, Pascal, and many others. The main paradigm here is that the computer is working for us, and we're telling it what to do by giving explicit instructions. For example:

```
CMP AX, BX
JNAE greater
MOV CX, BX
RET
greater:
MOV CX, AX
RET
```

This is an Assembly "sub-routine" for the Intel 8086 processor. It finds and returns the maximum between two integers. We put them into `AX` and `BX`, respectively, and the result appears in `CX`. Here is exactly the same code in C:

```
int max(int a, int b) {
  if (a > b) {
    return a;
  }
  return b;
}
```

What's so wrong with that, you may ask. Nothing. There is nothing wrong with this code; it works perfectly. This is actually how all computers work. They expect us to give them instructions, which they will execute one by one. That's how we have been writing software for years. The advantage of this approach is that we stay close to the CPU, always directing it where to go next. We are in charge, and the computer follows our instructions. We tell the computer how to find the maximum number out of two. We decide, it follows. And the flow is always sequential, from the top of the script to the bottom.

This *sequential* type of thinking is called "thinking as a computer." A computer starts to execute instructions at some point and stops at another point. When writing C code, we're forced to think like that. Statements go from top to bottom, and they are separated by semicolons. This style is inherited from Assembly.

Even though languages higher than Assembly have procedures, sub-routines, packages, modules, and other mechanisms of abstraction, they don't eliminate the sequential nature of thinking. We still go from the top to the bottom. There is nothing wrong with this approach for small software, but on a bigger scale, it is hard to think like this.

Take a look at the same code in Lisp, which is a *functional* programming language:

```
(defun max (a b)
  (if (> a b) a b))
```

Can you tell where execution starts and where it ends here? Not really. We don't know how the CPU will calculate the result or how exactly that function `if` will work. We are very "detached" from the CPU. We are now thinking as functions, not as a computer. When we need a new "thing", we define it:

```
(def x (max 5 9))
```

We *define* rather than give instructions to the CPU. In this line, we bind `x` to `(max 5 9)`. We don't ask the computer to calculate the maximum. We just say that `x` "is a" maximum of these two numbers. How it will be calculated and when it is out of our control. Pay attention, this is important—`x` "is a" maximum. This "is a" is what differentiates functional, logical, and object-oriented programming from procedural programming.

In computer thinking, we are in charge, and we control the flow of the execution of instructions. In object-oriented thinking, we just define who is who and let them interact when they need to. Here is how this maximum calculation must look in OOP:

```
class Max implements Number {
  private final Number a;
  private final Number b;
  public Max(Number left, Number right) {
    this.a = left;
    this.b = right;
  }
}
```

This is how I would use it:

```
Number x = new Max(5, 9);
```

You see, I'm not calculating the maximum. I'm just defining that
`x` "is a" maximum between five and nine. I don't really care
what is inside that object of class `Max` and how exactly it
implements interface `Number`. I don't give my CPU any
instructions about that calculation. I'm just instantiating an
object. This is very similar to `def` in Lisp. In this aspect, OOP
is very similar to functional programming.

To the contrary, static methods in OOP are exactly what
sub-routines are in C or Assembly. They have nothing to do with
OOP and encourage us to write procedural code in
object-oriented syntax. This is Java code:

```
int x = Math.max(5, 9);
```

This is terribly wrong and must not be used in proper
object-oriented design.

3.2.2 Declarative vs. imperative style

Imperative programming "describes computation in terms of
statements that change a program's state." *Declarative*
programming, on the other hand, "expresses the logic of a
computation without describing its control flow" (I'm quoting
Wikipedia). This is pretty much what we talked about on the
previous few pages. Imperative programming resembles what
computers do—it executes operations one by one. Declarative
programming is closer to the natural thinking paradigm, where
we have "entities" and "relations" between them. Obviously,
declarative programming is a much more powerful approach, but
imperative is much easier for a procedural programmer to
understand. Why is declarative more powerful? Stay with me,

and in a few pages we'll get there.

But what does all this have to do with static methods? No matter if it is a static method or an object, we still have to ask `if (a > b)` somewhere, right? Yes, that's right. Both a static method and an object just wrap around an actual `if` statement that does the job of comparing `a` to `b`. But the difference is in how that functionality *is used* by other classes, objects, and methods. And this difference is crucial. Let's see it through an example.

Say I have an interval between two integers, and I have another integer that has to be in that interval. I want to make sure it's there. This is what I *have* to do if method `max()` is static:

```
public static int between(int l, int r, int x) {
  return Math.min(Math.max(l, x), r);
}
```

I have to create another static method, `between()`, which uses two existing static methods, `Math.min()` and `Math.max()`. This is the only way I can do this. And it is an imperative-style operation, because the calculation happens right here when it's needed. When I call it, I get it immediately:

```
int y = Math.between(5, 9, 13); // 9 returned
```

I get number `9` right when I call method `between()`. My CPU will work on this calculation when the call is made. It is *imperative*. What is declarative, then? Here it is:

```
class Between implements Number {
  private final Number num;
  Between(Number left, Number right, Number x) {
    this.num = new Min(new Max(left, x), right);
  }
  @Override
  public int intValue() {
    return this.num.intValue();
  }
}
```

Here is how I will use it:

```
Number y = new Between(5, 9, 13); // not yet!
```

Do you see the difference? It is crucial. This style is *declarative*, because I don't tell my CPU to calculate the number yet. I just define what *it is* and let the user of variable `y` decide when to calculate its `intValue()`, if ever. Maybe it will never be calculated and my CPU will never know that the number is `9`. All I did is merely declare what `y` is. I just declared. I didn't instruct my CPU to do anything yet. As the definition above says, I expressed the logic without describing its control.

I hear you saying, "OK, I got it; there are two approaches (declarative and imperative), but why is the first one better than the second one?". I mentioned above that it's "obvious" that the declarative one is more powerful, but I didn't say why. Now that both approaches are illustrated by example, let's discuss the advantages of the declarative one.

First of all, it's faster. Well, at first glance, it is slower. But if you look closer, you will see that it's actually *faster*, because performance optimization is under our tight control. Indeed, making an instance of class `Between` is a more time-consuming

operation than making a call to the static method
`between()`—at least in most programming languages at the
time of this writing. I truly hope that in the near future, we'll
have a language where object instantiation will be as quick as a
method call. But we are not there yet. That's why the
declarative approach is slower... if the execution path is
straightforward and simple.

If it's just a single call to a single static method, there's no doubt
it is faster than making an instance of an object and then calling
its methods. But if and when we have many static methods, they
will all be called in order to complete the task rather than work
on only the results we actually need, as is what happens with
objects. How about this:

```
public void doIt() {
  int x = Math.between(5, 9, 13);
  if (/* Do we need it? */) {
    System.out.println("x=" + x);
  }
}
```

In this example, we calculate `x` whether we need it or not. The
CPU will find out that the number is `9` in both cases. Is the
following method as fast as this one, using a declarative
approach?

```
public void doIt() {
  Integer x = new Between(5, 9, 13);
  if (/* Do we need it? */) {
    System.out.println("x=" + x);
  }
}
```

I think that the declarative one is faster. It is more optimized. It
doesn't tell the CPU to calculate everything. Instead, it lets the

CPU decide *when and where* the result is actually needed, and the calculation happens on demand.

The point is that the declarative approach is faster because it's more *optimal*. This is the first argument in favor of declarative over imperative programming styles in OOP. Actually, there is absolutely no place for the imperative style in OOP, and performance optimization is the first reason. It goes without saying that the more control we have over optimization in our code, the more maintainable it is. Instead of letting the compiler, a virtual machine, or a CPU optimize the execution flow, we do it at the source code level.

The second reason is *polymorphism*. Simply put, polymorphism is the ability to break dependencies between code blocks. Let's say I want to change the algorithm of that number-in-interval calculation. It is very primitive as it is, but I want to change it. I don't want it to use classes `Max` and `Min`. I want it to do a comparison using `if-then-else` statements. This is how I can do that with a declarative approach:

```
class Between implements Number {
  private final Number num;
  Between(int left, int right, int x) {
    this(new Min(new Max(left, x), right));
  }
  Between(Number number) {
    this.num = number;
  }
}
```

It's the exact same class `Between` that I mentioned a few minutes before, but with an extra ctor. Now, I can use it with a different algorithm:

```
Integer x = new Between(
  new IntegerWithMyOwnAlgorithm(5, 9, 13)
);
```

That's maybe not the best example because class `Between` is very primitive, but I hope you get the idea. It is very easy to decouple class `Between` from classes `Max` and `Min`, because *they are classes*. In object-oriented programming, an object is a first-class citizen, while a static method is not. We can pass an object as an argument to a ctor, while a static method can't be used this way[1]. In OOP, objects are linked to objects, they talk to objects, and they exchange data with other objects. To make an object absolutely decoupled from all other objects, we just need to make sure it doesn't use `new` operators in any of its methods (see 3.6) and in its primary ctor (see 1.2).

Let me reiterate: To make an object fully decoupled from all other objects, you just have to make sure operator `new` is not used anywhere in its methods or its primary ctor.

Can you make the same decoupling and refactoring operation with this imperative piece of code?

```
int y = Math.between(5, 9, 13);
```

No, you can't. Static method `between()` uses two static methods, `min()` and `max()`, and you can't do anything about it without fully re-writing it. And how will you be able to re-write it? Pass a new static method as a fourth parameter? How ugly would that be? Pretty much.

---

[1] Well, we can do this in many languages, including Java8, Ruby, PHP, and Python, but this feature has nothing to do with object-oriented programming. It is a surrogate of procedural and functional programming that exists in all popular languages just because it is "convenient." In reality, it only increases the confusion.

That was my second argument in favor of the declarative programming style—It makes objects less coupled, and does this in a very elegant way. Needless to say, less coupling leads to more maintainability.

The third reason why declarative is better than imperative is expressiveness—Declarative talks about results, while imperative explains one way to do it. The latter is way less intuitive than the former. I have to "execute" the code in my head first in order to understand what result to expect. This is imperative:

```
Collection<Integer> evens = new LinkedList<>();
for (int number : numbers) {
  if (number % 2 == 0) {
    evens.add(number);
  }
}
```

In order to understand what this code is doing, I have to go through it. I have to "visualize" this loop. I basically have to do what the CPU does—go through the array of numbers and put even ones into a new list. Here is how the same algorithm would look in a declarative style:

```
Collection<Integer> evens = new Filtered(
  numbers,
  new Predicate<Integer>() {
    @Override
    public boolean suitable(Integer number) {
      return number % 2 == 0;
    }
  }
);
```

This code is much closer to English than the previous one. It literally reads as "`evens` is a filtered collection where only those numbers that are even are included." I don't know exactly how class `Filtered` builds this collection—whether it uses a `for` statement or something else. All I need to know here, while reading this code, is the fact that the collection is "filtered." The implementation details are hidden, while the behavior is expressed.

I realize that for some of you reading this book now, the first snippet may look easier to read. It is a bit shorter, and it is very similar to what you see every day in source code around you. I want to assure you that it's a matter of habit. It's a misleading feeling. Start thinking in terms of *objects* and their *behavior* instead of *algorithms* and their *execution*, and you will get the right feeling. A declarative style is precisely about objects and behavior, while an imperative one is about algorithms and execution.

If that code still looks ugly to you, try Groovy, for example:

```
def evens = new Filtered(
  numbers,
  { Integer number -> number % 2 == 0 }
);
```

The fourth reason is code *cohesion*. Look at the previous two snippets again. Pay attention to the fact that in the second one, we declare `evens` in a single statement, which is `evens = Filtered(...)`. This means that all lines of code responsible for the "calculation" of this collection stay together and can't be separated by a mistake. To the contrary, in the first snippet, there is no obvious "glue" between the lines. One can easily change their order by mistake and the algorithm will break.

With such a simple piece of code, it's not a big problem, as the algorithm is obvious. But with a bigger piece of imperative code, like one with, say, 50 lines, we may have a hard time understanding which lines are coupled together. We discussed this problem of "temporal coupling" a few pages before, in Section 2.6.3, while talking about immutable objects. The declarative programming style also helps get rid of that coupling, and thanks to that, it increases maintainability.

There are probably more reasons, but I listed the most important ones as I see them in relation to OOP. I hope I've managed to convince you that declarative style is the way to go. Some of you may say, "Yes, I get the idea, and I will combine declarative and imperative styles where they fit best. I will use objects when it makes sense and static methods when I need to do something small and fast, like calculate the maximum out of two integers." My answer is, "No, you're wrong!" We shouldn't combine them. We should never use imperative style. And it's not a dogma. There is a very practical reason behind this.

Imperative style technically can't be combined with declarative. Once you start using imperative, you're doomed to stay with it, and eventually your entire code base will become imperative.

Let's say we have two static methods: `max()` and `min()`. They do something very small and quick, so we make them static. Now, we want to create a bigger "algorithm" to put the number into an interval. We want to go the declarative route. We want to create class `Between` instead of static method `between()`. Can we? We probably can in a surrogate way, but we can't do it properly, as explained above. We can't use constructors and encapsulation. We have to make direct, explicit, static method calls right inside our new class `Between`. In other words, we can't write pure, clean object-oriented code if reusable components are static methods.

130

Static methods are like a *cancer* in object-oriented software—once you let them get a toe-hold, it's very difficult to get rid of them and their presence will only grow. Just stay away from them in the first place.

"But I've got them everywhere!"—you may say—"What to do?." Well, what can I say... you're in trouble, like all of us. We have tons of open source libraries almost entirely made of utility classes (we'll discuss them in the next Section) and static methods. Like with a tumor, the best cure is a knife. Just don't use that software, if you can afford not to. However, in most cases you won't be able to afford a knife, since the libraries are very popular and provide really useful functionality. In that case, your best option is to isolate that tumor by creating your own classes that wrap static methods in order to let your code deal with objects. For example, there is a static method `FileUtils.readLines()` in Apache Commons, which reads all lines from a text file. Here is how we can turn it into an object:

```
class FileLines implements Iterable<String> {
  private final File file;
  public Iterator<String> iterator() {
    return Arrays.asList(
      FileUtils.readLines(this.file)
    ).iterator();
  }
}
```

Now, in order to read all lines from a text file, our software will do this:

```
Iterable<String> lines = new FileLines(f);
```

The static method call will happen only inside the class `FileLines` and eventually we'll be able to get rid of it. Or maybe this will never happen. But the point is that we won't have static method calls anywhere in our code. Well, just in one place, inside class `FileLines`. That's how we isolate the deceased and deal with it incrementally.

3.2.3 Utility classes

A so-called "utility" class is not really a class but a collection of static methods used by other methods for convenience (they are also known as "helpers"). For example, class `java.lang.Math` is a classic example of a utility class. These "creatures" are very popular in Java, Ruby, and almost every modern language, unfortunately. Why aren't they classes? Because they don't instantiate objects. In Section 1.1, we discussed the difference between an object and a class, and agreed that a class is a "factory of objects." A utility class is not a factory of anything. Here is an example:

```
class Math {
  private Math() {
    // intentionally empty
  }
  public static int max(int a, int b) {
    if (a < b) {
      return b;
    }
    return a;
  }
}
```

It is a good practice, for those who use utility classes, to create a private ctor like in this example to avoid instantiation of the "class." Because the ctor is private, nobody can make an instance of the class except its own methods.

Utility classes are a triumph of procedural programmers in the OOP domain. A utility class is not just a bad thing, as a static method is, but an aggregation of bad things. Every bad word I've said above about static methods can be said here again, but with a multiplied emphasis. Utility classes are a terrible anti-pattern in OOP. Stay away from them.

3.2.4 Singleton Pattern

The Singleton Pattern is a very popular concept that looks like a replacement of static methods. Indeed, there is only one static method, and a singleton looks almost like a real object. However, it's not:

```
class Math {
  private static Math INSTANCE = new Math();
  private Math() {}
  public static Math getInstance() {
    return Math.INSTANCE;
  }
  public int max(int a, int b) {
    if (a < b) {
      return b;
    }
    return a;
  }
}
```

This is a very typical example of a singleton. There is only one instance of class `Math`, and its name is `INSTANCE`. Anyone can gain access to it just by calling `getInstance()`. The constructor is `private` in order to prevent direct instantiations of objects from this class. The only way to gain access to `INSTANCE` is by calling `getInstance()`.

Singleton is famous for being a "design pattern", while in reality it is a terrible *anti-pattern*. There are many reasons why it is a bad programming concept, and I will list a few of the most important ones in relation to static methods. Actually, it would be easier if we first discuss how a singleton is different from the utility class we just talked about. This is how a utility `Math` class would look, doing exactly the same as the singleton above:

```
class Math {
  private Math() {}
  public static int max(int a, int b) {
    if (a < b) {
      return b;
    }
    return a;
  }
}
```

This is how method `max()` will be utilized:

```
Math.max(5, 9); // utility class
Math.getInstance().max(5, 9); // singleton
```

What is the difference? It looks like the second line is just longer, while it does exactly the same. Why was the singleton invented if we already had static methods and utility classes? I often ask this question when I interview Java programmers. And the first answer I usually hear is that with a singleton, it's possible to encapsulate a state. For example:

```
class User {
  private static User INSTANCE = new User();
  private String name;
  private User() {}
  public static User getInstance() {
    return User.INSTANCE;
  }
  public String getName() {
    return this.name;
  }
  public String setName(String txt) {
    this.name = txt;
  }
}
```

That's a terrible piece of code, but I have to show it for the sake of argument. It's a singleton that literally means "user currently using the system." This approach is very popular in many web frameworks, where singletons exist for users, web sessions, etc. So a typical first answer to my question about the difference between a singleton and a utility class is that "a singleton preserves state." However, it's a wrong answer. The purpose of a singleton is not to preserve the state. Here is a utility class that does exactly the same as the singleton above:

```
class User {
  private static String name;
  private User() {}
  public static String getName() {
    return User.name;
  }
  public static String setName(String txt) {
    User.name = txt;
  }
}
```

This utility class preserves the state, and there is literally no difference between it and the singleton above. So, what is the big deal? What is the right answer? The only valid answer is that a singleton is a dependency that is possible to break, while a utility class is a hard-coded tight coupling that is impossible to break. In other words, the benefit of a singleton is the ability to add method `setInstance()` along with `getInstance()`. This is the right answer, though I rarely hear it. Let's say that this is my usage of a singleton:

```
Math.getInstance().max(5, 9);
```

My code is coupled with class `Math`. In other words, class `Math` is a *dependency* I'm relying upon. Without that class, my code won't work, and in order to test my code, I have to have class `Math` available to complete my requests. In the case of this particular class, it's not a big issue because it is rather primitive. However, if a singleton is big, I may need to "mock" it or just replace it with something more suitable for my testing purposes. Simply put, I don't want method `Math.max()` to be executed while a unit test is running. How can I do it? This is how:

```
Math math = new FakeMath();
Math.setInstance(math);
```

A Singleton Pattern allows me to replace the encapsulated static object, enabling testability of the entire concept. The right answer is that a singleton is much better than a utility class only because it lets us change the encapsulated object. In a utility class, there is no object—we can't change anything. A utility class is an unbreakable, hard-coded dependency—pure evil in OOP.

So where are we? A singleton is better than a utility class but is still an anti-pattern, and a terrible one at that. Why? Because logically and technically, a singleton is a *global variable*, no less and no more. And in OOP, there is no *global scope*. That's why there is no place for a global variable. This is C software with a variable in a global scope of visibility:

```
#include <stdio>
int line = 0;
void echo(char* text) {
  printf("[%d] %s\n", ++line, text);
}
```

Every time we call `echo()`, global variable `line` gets incremented. Technically, variable `line` is visible to every function and every line of code in this `.c` file. It is visible *globally*. Kudos to Java designers; they didn't copy this feature from C. In Java, as well as in Ruby and many other semi-OOP languages, global variables are not allowed. Why? Because they have nothing to do with OOP at all. It's a purely procedural feature. Global variables totally violate the idea of encapsulation. They are just bad. I don't think I need to explain that more in this book. I believe it is just obvious that global variables are a bad thing, along with `GOTO` operators.

However, despite all the reasons against global variables, someone[1] found a way to introduce them in Java, and thus invented the singleton. It's just an *abuse* of the object-oriented paradigm, and it became possible only because we had static methods. Static methods technically enabled that cheating.

Don't use singletons, ever. Don't even think about them.

---

[1] I don't know who it was exactly, but the singleton is described as a design pattern in Erich Gamma et. al., Design Patterns, Addison-Wesley, 1995 on page 128. Actually, I would recommend that you read this book, but with a good amount of skepticism.

What is the alternative, you may ask? If we do need something to be available to many classes across the entire software, what do we do? Say, we really need most of our classes to know who the user that is currently logged in is. We don't have utility classes and we don't have singletons. What do we have? Encapsulation! Just encapsulate that user in all objects that may need it.

Everything that your class needs for his work must be provided via his constructor and encapsulated inside. That's it. No exceptions. An object must never touch anything else, except his encapsulated properties. You may say that it will be necessary to encapsulate too much: database connections, logged in user, file storage, current session, command line arguments, etc. Yes, true, there will be too many if your class is too big and not cohesive enough. If you need to encapsulate too much, refactor the class and make it smaller, as we discussed in Section 2.1.

But never use a Singleton. There are no exceptions to this rule.

3.2.5 Functional programming

I hear this argument rather often: they say that if your objects are small and immutable, and you don't have static methods, why don't you just use functional programming (FP)? Indeed, there is a lot of similarity between functions and objects, if objects are as "elegant" as this book recommends. So why do we need objects? Why not just use Lisp, Clojure, or Haskell instead of Java and C++?

This is the class that represents a maximum of two integers, from Section 3.2.1:

```
class Max implements Number {
  private final int a;
  private final int b;
  public Max(int left, int right) {
    this.a = left;
    this.b = right;
  }
  @Override
  public int intValue() {
    return this.a > this.b ? this.a : this.b;
  }
}
```

This is how we're supposed to use it:

```
Number x = new Max(5, 9);
```

This is how we would design a function in Lisp that would do exactly the same:

```
(defn max
  (a b)
  (if (> a b) a b))
```

So, why use objects? The Lisp code is much shorter.

OOP is more expressive and powerful, because it has objects and methods, while FP only has functions. Some FP languages have objects, too, but I consider them OOP languages with FP elements, not the other way around. I also think that Lambda Expressions in Java, as a move towards FP, make Java less solid, because they distract us from true object-oriented style. FP is a great paradigm, but OOP is better. Especially if done right.

In an ideal OOP language, I think we would have classes and functions inside them. Not Java methods as micro-procedures, which we have now, but true functions in a pure FP paradigm with a single exit point. That would be an ideal situation.

3.2.6 Composable decorators

I think I made this term up. Composable decorators are just objects that wrap other objects. They are just decorators—a well-known design pattern—but they become *composable* when we start to compose them into multi-layer structures, for example:

```
names = new Sorted(
  new Unique(
    new Capitalized(
      new Replaced(
        new FileNames(
          new Directory(
            "/var/users/*.xml"
          )
        ),
        "([^.]+)\\.xml",
        "$1"
      )
    )
  )
);
```

This code looks very clean and object-oriented to me. It is purely declarative, as explained in Section 3.2.2. It doesn't "do" anything, but it does declare object `names` that *is a* sorted collection of unique capitalized strings representing file names in a directory, modified by a regular expression replacement. I just explained what this object is without saying a word about how it is built. I just *declared* it.

Do you find this code clean and easy to understand? I hope you do, taking into account everything we've discussed up to this point.

These are what I call composable decorators. The classes `Directory`, `FileNames`, `Replaced`, `Capitalized`, `Unique`, and `Sorted` are decorators because their behavior is entirely motivated by the objects they encapsulate. They add some behavior to the encapsulated objects. Their state is the same as the state of their objects.

Sometimes, but not necessarily, they expose the same interface as their encapsulated objects. For example, `Unique` is an `Iterable<String>`, and it also encapsulates an iterable of strings. However, `FileNames` is an iterable of strings, but it encapsulates an iterable of files.

The majority of code in properly designed object-oriented software must look like the code you see above. We have to compose decorators, one into another, and do almost nothing besides that. At some point of time, we call `app.run()` and this entire pyramid starts to react. There literally should be no procedural "statements" like `if`, `for`, `switch`, and `while`. This may sound like a utopia, but it is not.

Operator `if` is given to us by Java, and we use it in a procedural way, making statement after statement. Why can't some other language, which will eventually replace Java, give us class `If`. Instead of this procedural code:

```
float rate;
if (client.age() > 65) {
  rate = 2.5;
} else {
  rate = 3.0;
}
```

We would write this object-oriented code:

```
float rate = new If(
  client.age() > 65,
  2.5, 3.0
);
```

Even more, how about this:

```
float rate = new If(
  new Greater(client.age(), 65),
  2.5, 3.0
);
```

And now, the final improvement:

```
float rate = new If(
  new GreaterThan(
    new AgeOf(client),
    65
  ),
  2.5, 3.0
);
```

This is pure object-oriented and declarative code. It doesn't do anything, but only declares what `rate` is.

My point is that in pure OOP, we don't need operators inherited from procedural languages like C. We don't need `if`, `for`, `switch`, and `while`. We need classes `If`, `For`, `Switch`, and `While`. See the difference?

We haven't arrived at that language yet, but we'll get there sooner or later. I'm sure. In the meantime, try to stay away from long methods and complex procedures. Design micro classes, and make sure they are composable. Make sure they can be reused by other classes as elements of the composition of a bigger object.

I would say that object-oriented programming is the job of composing bigger objects from smaller ones.

But what does all this have to do with static methods? I'm sure you understand already—static methods are not composable in any way. They make everything I just explained and demonstrated impossible. We can't make bigger objects from smaller ones that have static methods. Static methods simply oppose the idea of composition. This is yet another reason why static methods are pure evil in OOP.

To conclude, don't use *static* keywords anywhere in your software and you will do yourself, and those who will reuse your code later, a big favor.

3.3 Never accept NULL arguments

Discuss at http://goo.gl/TzrYbz

NULL (a.k.a. `null` in Java, `nil` in Ruby, `NULL` in C++, `None` in Python, etc.) is yet another big problem in the object-oriented world, along with static methods (Section 3.2) and mutability (Section 2.6). In a nutshell, you're making a big mistake if you use `NULL` anywhere in your code. Anywhere—I mean it. Here, let's talk about `NULL` as an argument for a method. Later, in Section 4.1, we'll discuss `NULL` being returned as a result.

Consider this method design:

```
public Iterable<File> find(String mask) {
  // Go through the directory and
  // find all files that match the
  // mask provided; for example, "*.txt".
  // Retrieve all files if mask is NULL.
}
```

A very common approach is to allow users to provide `NULL` instead of a real object as a way of saying, "I don't have an object, so consider it absent." Indeed, it looks like a convenient alternative to these two methods:

```
public Iterable<File> findAll();
public Iterable<File> find(String mask);
```

Having a single method looks more compact and easier for a user to remember, right? I don't have to remember that if I need to filter by a mask, I call `find()`, while if I need all files instead, I have to use `findAll()`. If there are two methods, I can still remember them. But what if there are three arguments and each of them may be `NULL`? I will have to create nine different methods. Using `NULL` seems to be a much more convenient and compact approach.

It does sound logical, but it goes against the object paradigm, where each object is fully responsible for his own behavior.

In order to implement this `find()` method that accepts NULL, we will have to do something like this:

```
public Iterable<File> find(String mask) {
  if (mask == null) {
    // find all files
  } else {
    // find files by mask
  }
}
```

The evil component is this `mask==null` comparison. Instead of *talking* to object `mask`, we go around and *ignore* it. We are literally asking to his face, "Are you worth talking to?" or even, "Is he worth talking to?" We don't even talk to the object directly. We ask someone who is supposed to know whether he is good enough or not. That's not a very polite way of communicating, is it?

If we *respect* the object, we would do something like this:

```
public Iterable<File> find(Mask mask) {
  if (mask.empty()) {
    // find all files
  } else {
    // find files by mask
  }
}
```

Or, even better, like this:

```
public Iterable<File> find(Mask mask) {
  Collection<File> files = new LinkedList<>();
  for (File file : /* all files */)
    if (mask.matches(file)) {
      files.add(file);
    }
  }
  return files;
}
```

If we respected the object `mask`, we would let him decide whether he has something for us or if he is empty. We won't judge him by his face. We won't say that if you're `NULL`, we don't use you, but if you're a "real" object, we'll talk to you.

Accepting `NULL` as an argument inevitably forces us to use that `mask==null` comparison. We simply can't do otherwise. Every time, before working with an object, we have to check his "realness." And by checking it, we are taking a lot of responsibility from the object. We are turning him into a dumb data structure that is not capable of taking care of itself and always expects someone to put something into it and get something back.

In the world of procedural programming, where sub-routines manipulate data, the existence of `NULL` is also a bad idea, but it is a bit more explainable. I give you some data, and I don't expect you to *talk* to them. They are not smart enough to have a conversation with you. They are just bytes and bits. Technically, when I *give* you the data, I just give you an address in memory where you can find them. The address is called a *pointer*; for example, `0x89f4a328`. All bytes in memory are numbered, and this number is the position of the first byte in the data structure I'm trying to pass to you (in C):

```
#include <stdio.h>
void foo(char* p) {
  printf("Fifth byte is: %x", *(p + 5));
}
```

This `foo()` sub-routine will ask the CPU to go to that address in memory and fetch the fifth byte. But we have an agreement that if I give you `0x00000000` as an address, *you* won't ask the CPU to go there. That's simply because it's almost impossible that my data structure is located there. Well, it is never possible with current computer architecture. That's why all programmers agreed years ago that if a pointer is equal to zero, we call it `NULL` and never use it as a real address. We never ask the CPU to fetch anything from there (C again):

```
#include <stdio.h>
void foo(char* p) {
  if (p == 0) {
    printf("It's NULL; there is no data.");
  } else {
    printf("Fifth byte is: %x", *(p + 5));
  }
}
```

Remember, this is just a convention. Technically, there is no difference between a "real" pointer `0x89f4a328` and a not-so-real `0x00000000`, which we agreed to call `NULL` and treat in a special way.

What happens if I forget the agreement made many years ago and ask the CPU to retrieve some data from the address at position `0x00000000`? The result is unpredictable[1] in C, but in most cases, the CPU will catch me and terminate the execution

---

[1] I'm not a big expert on this, but a few reviewers told me that the result is very predictable here, the execution will definitely stop.

of the process with a "segmentation fault" message. This is how it works in the world of imperative procedural programming. You can try it yourself:

```
#include <stdio.h>
int main(int argc, char** argv) {
  char* p = 0;
  printf("Byte at zero: %x", *p); // fault here!
}
```

Unfortunately, the object-oriented world inherited this "concept" even though most languages don't have pointers anymore. We don't have pointers in Java, and we don't need to *de-reference* them. This is the name of the `*p` construct from the code above. A pointer is just an integer, a position in memory of the data I need. In order to tell the compiler that I want to work with the data, not with the address, I have to de-reference the pointer.

It's simpler than it sounds, though pointers are usually considered to be the biggest pain in C programming, mostly because they are counterintuitive. It's much easier for us to think about objects de-referenced automatically than about data structures that are located somewhere in memory. If we have objects and we don't have pointers, why do we have `null` in Java? Honestly, I don't know.

Moreover, I think it's a *big mistake* in Java design, as well as in Ruby, JavaScript, and many other object-oriented languages, even the most modern ones.

But what do we do if there is nothing to pass as an argument of method `find()`, you may ask. What if there is no `mask`, and we simply want to pass "nothing"? Why not use `null`?

In OOP, this problem of an "absent argument" must be solved by a so-called "null object." You don't have anything to give me?

Give me an object that behaves like it's empty. Don't put this problem on my shoulders by asking me to check whether you gave me an object or `NULL`. Instead, always give me an object, but in some situations give me a special object that will refuse to talk to me if I ask too much.

Let's say we have that `Mask` interface that is supposed to be passed to the method `find()` in order to tell which file matches the mask and which does not:

```
interface Mask {
  boolean matches(File file);
}
```

A proper implementation of this interface will encapsulate a "glob" pattern (for example, `"*.txt"`) and match file names against it. To the contrary, a null object would look like this:

```
class AnyFile implements Mask {
  @Override
  boolean matches(File file) {
    return true;
  }
}
```

This is a corner case of a mask—it doesn't have any logic inside. It just returns `true`, no matter what file we pass to it. Now, instead of passing `null` to the method `find()`, we just create an instance of class `AnyFile`, and that's it. The method `find()` will have no idea what's going on. It will still think that a proper mask is passed to it.

Let's say we agree that our methods never accept `NULL`. But what if their users send `NULL` anyway, despite the agreement made and the documentation saying, "please, no NULL here"? How should we react to that abusive behavior? There are basically two approaches: defensive or ignorant. In a defensive approach, we check and throw an exception if there is `NULL`:

```
public Iterable<File> find(Mask mask) {
  if (mask == null) {
    throw new IllegalArgumentException(
      "Mask can't be NULL; please provide an object."
    );
  }
  // Find files by mask and return
}
```

The second approach is ignorant, and I'm in favor of it. Just don't do anything and assume that the argument is not `NULL`. Sooner or later, when you start manipulating the argument, a `NullPointerException` will be thrown and the caller will understand his mistake.

Don't pollute your code with extra checks. `NullPointerException` is a proper indicator of an incorrectly passed `NULL` argument. There's no need to make it any smarter or more informative. There are no `NULL` references in properly designed software anyway. Don't be defensive, just ignore it and let the JVM handle these situations in a standard way.

To summarize: Never accept `NULL` as a method argument. No exceptions here. Never.

3.4 Be loyal and immutable, or cons[...]

`Discuss at http://goo.gl/2UKLds`

We have already spent more than a dozen pages on object immutability in Section 2.6, but now it's time to talk about it once more, mostly because there is a very big and common confusion that we have to try to clarify. A very often-spoken argument against immutability is that the world is naturally mutable, and it's impossible to represent it with the help of only immutable objects. Indeed, we have input/output entities like files, streams, web pages, buffers, etc. All of them are essentially mutable and the most anticipated implementation of them is mutable.

Even though there is a lot of common sense in that, I disagree. Yes, the world is mutable, but that doesn't mean we can't model it with immutable objects. The confusion here is caused by our misunderstanding of *state* and *data*, which are two different things. As usual, let's start with an example:

```
class WebPage {
  private final URI uri;
  WebPage(URI path) {
    this.uri = path;
  }
  public String content() {
    // Makes HTTP GET request, loads web page
    // content, and converts it to UTF-8 string
  }
}
```

What do you think? Is he an immutable object or a mutable one? Does he look like a mutable one for you? If so, think again. In a nutshell, even though method `content()` may return different values on every subsequent call, the object is *immutable*. Because he doesn't change his state over his entire lifetime, it doesn't matter how he behaves and what data his methods return. And that is what probably confuses most of you.

Intuitively, we expect an immutable object to act as a *constant*, returning the same data every time we touch him. We think that if an object is immutable, he must behave like a string literal or a number. Indeed, most immutable classes in Java and other languages do behave like constants: `String`, `URI`, or `Double`, for example. Once you instantiate one of those classes, the object will be 100% predictable, and all his methods will always return the same. This is what we expect from an immutable object by definition, and it is wrong. Well, it is not entirely wrong, but it is an incomplete picture. It is just a corner case of immutability.

An immutable object is much more than that. The class `WebPage` is also immutable, even though its method `content()` is not predictable. We don't know what to expect from it, since it communicates with a real-life entity: a web page. What the method will retrieve through HTTP is not forecastable at all. That's why class `WebPage` doesn't look similar to class `String`, but it is also immutable. Even though his behavior is not predictable, the object is immutable. Even though the object is not constant, he is immutable, because he is "loyal" to the entity he represents.

Did I confuse you enough? To clarify, I need to start from scratch and define what a state is and what an object is. Bear with me. I will try to make it clear now.

An object is a *representative* of a real-life entity, like a file on disk, a web page, an array of bytes, a hash map, or a current calendar month. By real-life, we mean everything outside the scope of visibility for an object. For example, object `f` represents a file on disk:

```
public void echo() {
  File f = new File("/tmp/test.txt");
  System.out.println("File size: %d", file.length());
}
```

The scope of visibility here is defined by the "borders" of method `echo()`. In order to talk to a file on disk and ask about its size, we have to communicate with object `f` and its method `length()`. Object `f` is a representative of the file `/tmp/test.txt`. He represents its interests in front of us. He *is* a file, as far as it concerns us, inside method `echo()`.

In order to communicate with a file on disk, the object has to know its *coordinates*. These coordinates are also known as the object *state*. For example, in an object of class `WebPage`, the state is the URI of the page. In order to load its content, the object will communicate with the world through HTTP protocol, using URI as a coordinate of the HTTP end point. In class `File`, the state is the full path of the file in the file system. An example of this is `/tmp/test.txt`.

Basically, there are three elements in every object: identity, state, and behavior. Identity is what distinguishes `f` from other objects, state is what `f` knows about the file on disk, and behavior is what `f` can do for us on request. The main difference between immutable and mutable objects is that an immutable one doesn't have an identity and its state never changes. More precisely, immutable objects' identities are exactly the same as their states.

Look at the class `WebPage` above once again. If I make two

153

instances of this class with the same `uri`, will they be different from each other? Will they expose different behavior? No. They will be `identical`, because their encapsulated states are equal to each other. They will both represent the same real-life web page. That's why there won't be any difference in which of them I'm talking to—I will still communicate with the same web page. The coordinates of the web page will be identical; that's why the objects will be identical, even though they are instantiated separately. A perfect implementation of a class as a factory of objects (see Section 1.1) should understand that and avoid duplicate instances, which encapsulate the same state.

However, in most OOP languages, including Java, this is not the case. By default, each object has its own unique identity, which can be overriden. For example, I would define it like this for our class `WebPage` (it is a pseudo implementation; a real `equals()` method would be a bit more complex):

```
class WebPage {
  private final URI uri;
  WebPage(URI path) {
    this.uri = path;
  }
  @Override
  public void equals(Object obj) {
    return this.uri.equals(
      WebPage.class.cast(obj).uri
    );
  }
  @Override
  public int hashCode() {
    return this.uri.hashCode();
  }
}
```

As you see, both methods `equals()` and `hashCode()` rely on the encapsulated property `uri`, making objects of class `WebPage` transparent—they don't have their own identity anymore. They represent a page on the web, and their only state is the coordinates of that page, in the form of a URI.

On the other hand, mutable objects are a whole different story. They allow for modification of their state, which requires an identity apart from their state. In a perfect object-oriented world, we would have only immutable objects, and we would not need these two methods, `equals()` and `hashCode()`. They would be the same in all classes. There would be no need to define or redefine them. In an immutable class, all objects are identifiable by the state they encapsulate. The state is necessary and sufficient to identify an immutable object.

An immutable object knows where a real-life object is located and how to use it. That's it. He knows the coordinates, and we call them a *state*. I hope that's logical, at least for the example provided. When we're talking about a web page or a file, it's all clear because the real world is truly "real." Its entities are somewhere outside of our software. That's why it is easy to separate the entity and its representative.

In other words, an immutable object is *loyal* to the real-life entity it represents. He never changes the coordinates of that entity. He always works with the same entity, no matter what. That's why I'm saying that he is *loyal*. A mutable object, on the other hand, can change the coordinates of the entity he is working with. That's why he is not loyal.

What should we do in the case of a collection of numbers? The task is trivial, and I want to have a collection of integers from which I can add or remove elements, iterate existing elements, count them, etc. How can I do this with only immutable objects? There are two possible options: a *constant* list or an *immutable* list. Here is the constant:

```
class ConstantList<T> {
  private final T[] array;
  ConstantList() {
    this(new T[0]);
  }
  private ConstantList(T[] numbers) {
    this.array = numbers;
  }
  ConstantList with(T number) {
    T[] nums = new T[this.array.length + 1];
    System.arraycopy(
      this.array, 0, nums,
      0, this.array.length
    );
    nums[this.array.length] = number;
    return new ConstantList(nums);
  }
  Iterable<T> iterate() {
    return Arrays.asList(this.array);
  }
}
```

This is how I would use it:

```
ConstantList list = new ConstantList()
  .with(1) // new object
  .with(15) // another object
  .with(5); // yet another object
```

I hope you understand how that works. On every attempt to modify the list and add a new element to it, a new list is created where all elements from the existing list are copied.

This is a classic immutable object, but I'm suggesting you call it a "constant" instead, because it is simply a corner case of immutability, where its state is equal to the real-life entity. Yes, the state `this.array` is *the same* as the entity which object `list` is representing. The object is representing an array, and the state itself *is* the array. Compare this class with the `WebPage` from a few pages ago. In that case, `this.uri` is just a coordinate of a real-world entity, a web page. On the other hand, here in `ConstantList`, the entity we represent is the state itself. Again, it is just a corner case.

Here is how I would make an immutable list:

```
class ImmutableList<T> {
  private final List<T> items = LinkedList<T>();
  void add(T number) {
    this.items.add(number);
  }
  Iterable<T> iterate() {
    return Collections.unmodifiableList(this.items);
  }
}
```

Does it look immutable to you? It looks like objects of this class can be modified; that's why they are mutable, right? No, not exactly. Let's try to analyze. Indeed, we can modify—but not the object. Look at the class `WebPage` again. What if we add a new method to it:

```
class WebPage {
  private final URI uri;
  WebPage(URI path) {
    this.uri = path;
  }
  public void modify(String content) {
    // Makes HTTP PUT request and modifies
    // the content of the web page.
  }
}
```

Did we just make it mutable? Definitely not. What is happening when we use it like this?

```
WebPage page = new WebPage("http://localhost:8080");
page.modify("<html/>");
```

Do we mutate the state of object `page`? No. Is this object still immutable? Absolutely. Is the web page it represents immutable? We don't know, but most likely not.

This situation is very similar to what we have in `ImmutableList`, but with a small difference—the real-life entity is *in memory*, not on the web. If Java design would be different, we would never see that difference. If Java would have a class `Memory`, we would design `ImmutableList` like this:

```
class ImmutableList<Integer> {
  private final Memory total =
    new Memory(2); // 2 bytes in heap
  private final Memory items =
    new Memory(100); // 100 bytes in heap
  void add(Integer number) {
    int pos = this.total.read();
    this.items.store(pos, number);
    this.total.store(pos + 1);
  }
}
```

It's a very primitive example, but I hope you understand what's going on there.

What do you think now? Does it look similar to `WebPage`? I think it does. The encapsulated objects `this.total` and `this.items` are the state. They are the coordinates of a few bytes in memory for the counter of list items, and a bit more bytes where the numbers are stored. The memory, or the web, or the disk are all the same for us, conceptually speaking. Our objects just represent them, nothing else.

This looks very similar to the concept of a pointer in C/C++. This is how that immutable list would look in C++:

```
#include <stdlib.h>
class ImmutableList {
public:
  ImmutableList() :
    total((int*) calloc(1, sizeof(int))),
    items((int*) malloc(100)) { }
  ~ImmutableList() {
    free(total);
    free(items);
  }
  void add(int number) {
    int pos = *total;
    items[pos] = number;
    *total = pos + 1;
  }
private:
  int* const total;
  int* const items;
};
```

Pay attention to the fact that both pointers `total` and `items` are constant. They are initialized in the ctor, where portions of memory are allocated and released when portions of memory are freed.

My point is that memory, conceptually, must be treated exactly the same way we treat a disk, network, or any other "external" storage. The language must provide built-in instruments for manipulating memory, but these instruments must be more powerful and flexible than C/C++ pointers. The problem with pointers is that they are too simple. They redirect us straight to the place in memory and make memory allocation our problem and responsibility. As you see in the example above, we have to `malloc()` a fixed number of bytes. What will we do when the entire memory chunk is occupied by items? We will need to extend the memory capacity, but we can't do it. We have to `malloc()` a new block of bytes, copy everything from the existing one into it, and then `free()` the existing one. This three-step procedure must be implemented by a built-in `Memory` class. Unfortunately, we don't have that in Java.

A chunk of bytes in memory is exactly the same kind of external resource for us as a file on disk. There is absolutely no difference, design-wise. Keeping this principle in mind, we can use immutable objects everywhere. Some of them will be constant, while others will just be immutable, representing portions of memory.

Obviously, it is better to use constant objects because they are easier to design, maintain, and understand. Almost everything said about immutable objects in Section 2.6 was about constant objects, which are corner cases of immutable ones.

Thus, any system, regardless of its business and technical domains, can and must be designed entirely from immutable objects, including games, desktop apps, mobile apps, web apps, enterprise systems, etc.

3.5 Never use getters and setters

Discuss at http://goo.gl/LSyvo9

Getters and setters: I don't know whether they're a pattern or just a convention. I'm sure you know what they are about, but let me remind you anyway. This is what they look like:

```
class Cash {
  private int dollars;
  public int getDollars() {
    return this.dollars;
  }
  public void setDollars(int value) {
    this.dollars = value;
  }
}
```

What do we have here? It is a mutable class with a single private property that is exposed to its users through *getter* `getDollars()`, and is modifiable through *setter* `setDollars()`. We already discussed in Section 2.6 that all classes must be immutable. This one is mutable. Furthermore, we discussed in Section 2.4 how methods must be named. This class has two incorrectly named methods. Also, this class doesn't have any constructors, which is against the principles we discussed in Section 2.1. My point is that this class already conflicts with the ideas I'm expressing in this book.

However, that's not all. Mutability, method names, and a complete absence of constructors are nothing compared to the much bigger sin this class is guilty of. It is not class, but rather a *data structure*. And this sin can't be forgiven. Amen.

3.5.1 Objects vs. data structures

What is the difference between an object and a data structure and why is being a data structure a sin in OOP?

Let's discuss the difference first. This is a data structure, in C:

```
struct Cash {
  int dollars;
}
```

This is a very similar thing, called an object, in C++:

```
#include <string>
class Cash {
public:
  Cash(int v): dollars(v) {};
  std::string print() const;
private:
  int dollars;
};
```

What is the difference? Let's see. This is how we're supposed to use the `cash` data structure, in C:

```
printf("Cash value is %d", cash.dollars);
```

This is how we would do something similar with an object of class `Cash`, in C++:

```
printf("Cash value is %s", cash.print());
```

See the difference? In the case of a `struct`, we directly access its member, `dollars`, and treat it as an integer. We don't do anything with the `struct`. We don't communicate with it. We directly access its member. The `struct` is just a *data bag* for us, without any "personality."

163

A `class` is something different. It doesn't allow us to touch its members in any way. Moreover, it doesn't show us its members. We don't even know that there is a member called `dollars` inside it. All we can do is ask the object to `print()` itself. How this happens, we don't know. Will any encapsulated members be involved? We don't know. This is what is called *encapsulation*, and this is what OOP is about.

Data structures are transparent, while objects are solid. Data structures are glass boxes, while objects are black boxes. Data structures are passive, while objects are active. Data structures are dead, while objects are alive. Good slogans, aren't they? I wanted to stop here and continue talking about getters and setters, assuming that objects are just better than data structures. That fact is obvious to everybody. However, I took a pause and tried to answer this myself: why is it that data structures are wrong? Why can't we have objects *and* data structures? Yes, objects are better, but why only them? Sometimes we simply need a plain old data structure with a few members inside. Why make an object with behavior, identity, and state? We're not OOP fanatics, are we?

No, we are not, but we do want to work only with objects and never with data structures, and there is a very rational and practical reason behind this.

As usual, it's all about maintainability. The main goal of each and every programming style, be it a procedural, functional, or object-oriented one, is to *simplify* things by *shrinking* the scope of visibility. The smaller the scope you have to understand at any particular moment, the more maintainable the software is and the easier it is to understand and modify.

In procedural and imperative programming, where the code

manipulates the data, the best way to simplify things is to use sub-routines and data aggregates. Instead of going through thousands of statements, we put a few of them aside, give them a name, and call it a sub-routine. Instead of managing hundreds of bytes, we group them into an array or a data structure and refer to it by a single pointer.

A group of bytes that stay together is convenient when we want to address them individually, just by adding a position to the location of the first byte. Such a group is easier to pass as an argument to a sub-routine. Instead of passing 10 different arguments to a structure, we pass it a pointer and the sub-routine finds all necessary bytes very easily.

The driving forces in this scenario are the code, the sub-routine, and the CPU instructions. They manipulate the data, and the data just sits and waits until someone changes or reads it.

In Section 3.2.1, we discussed the difference between procedural and object-oriented programming, and agreed that OOP was primarily invented in order to make things simpler than they were in the procedural world. Objects turned everything *upside down*. The code became passive, while data became active. Well, that was the intention of OOP, if I understand it right. Data do not sit and wait anymore. Instead, data are now encapsulated inside objects, and objects are "alive." They are wired to each other, and when it's time to do something, they trigger execution through messages, also known as method calls. In OOP, code doesn't dominate data. Instead, we let objects trigger code execution when necessary. This may sound too abstract, but that's the best explanation I have. Abstract or not, it is important to understand this fundamental difference between procedural and object-oriented styles. The code is not the king anymore. The code is a secondary element in OOP. Objects are first-class citizens, and their *initialization* through constructors *is* the software. Not operators or statements, but constructors.

Every time we try to use anything more complex than a byte in OOP, we take a step back to procedural programming. When we group a few bytes into a data structure and start using it to communicate between objects, we seriously compromise the entire object model of our application and there is almost no way back. We start thinking in terms of statements and operators, not objects and constructors. We already discussed the difference between imperative and declarative styles in Section 3.2.2. Now it's time to mention it all again. When data become more complex than a single byte, we're getting back into imperative programming. We simply have to write statements and operators that will manipulate those bytes, and these manipulations will inevitably be imperative.

To stay object-oriented and declarative, we have to hide data inside objects and never expose it to the outside. Only the object must know what exactly is encapsulated and how complex the structure of the data is. I would even say that we should not keep our data *naked*. We should always dress them properly. Nobody should be able to see them naked or touch them.

Thus, a very practical reason for choosing objects instead of data structures is that naked data encourages us to use a procedural programming style, which we want to avoid in OOP at all costs.

3.5.2 Good intentions, bad outcome

Getters and setters are designed to *violate* the principle of encapsulation, even though they declare the opposite.

They were introduced in Java in order to turn classes into data structures because Java didn't have such a thing by design. C++ has structures. That's why getters and setters are not required there. In Java, we need them in order to make objects that look like objects but are in reality passive data structures, just like `struct` in C++.

Well, we can turn a class into a data structure by just making its properties `public` (this is Java):

```
class Cash {
  public int dollars;
}
```

However, this would violate the basic rules of Java programming so deeply that everybody would tell you that you don't know what OOP is about. That's why, to avoid this public embarrassment, we all agreed to make properties private and attach setters and getters to all of them. Every modern IDE has a feature that adds setters and getters to an existing private property. You just select a class member, click a button, and get two new methods in the class, one prefixed with `get` and another one with `set`.

In Ruby, we have a built-in feature that creates setters and getters automatically. They are called accessors and mutators. We just say that we need them by using the `attr_reader` and `attr_writer` keywords:

```
class Cash
  attr_reader :dollars
  attr_writer :dollars
end
```

This is just a convenient replacement for the more verbose construct:

```
class Cash
  def dollars
    @dollars
  end
  def dollars=(value)
    @dollars = value
  end
end
```

Language and IDE designers encourage us to decorate private properties with getters and setters.

My point is that getters and setters are a convenient instrument for violating the principle of encapsulation in OOP. They look like methods, but in reality, they are just masking the ugly reality: we are getting direct access to data. The data are *naked*.

You may argue that the data are not naked, because getters and setters are methods. We can add some extra logic to them, validate the data, even change the way we store the data and retrieve it, but all this doesn't matter. On the surface, getters and setters look exactly like data access entry points to the user of the object. The object looks like a data structure, with bytes and bits inside. No matter what is inside the implementation of your getters and setters, they are data and they represent data, not behavior.

3.5.3 It's all about prefixes

It is important to mention that the evil part of this getters and setters anti-pattern is these two prefixes, `get` and `set`. They send us a clear message that the object is not really an object, but rather a data structure that doesn't anticipate any respect from us. It expects us to treat it as a collection of bytes, naked data. It doesn't want us to talk to it. It wants us to just inject some data into it and retrieve it back out.

It is totally fine to have a method that returns some data. For example:

```
class Cash {
  private final int value;
  public int dollars() {
    return this.value;
  }
}
```

But this name is not acceptable:

```
class Cash {
  private final int value;
  public int getDollars() {
    return this.value;
  }
}
```

Am I being too obsessive about naming here? Not at all. The difference is fundamental and very important. `getDollars()` is saying, "Go into your data, find dollars, and return it", while `dollars()` is asking, "How many dollars do you have?" See the difference? In the second case, I'm not treating the object as a storage of data. I respect him. I need to know how many dollars are there, but I don't assume that these dollars are stored there as private property. I make no assumptions about its internal organization and definitely don't think about him as a data structure.

The data are not naked in the first case, while in the second they are. They are totally exposed to the surface, and every single user of this class will see them.

The bottom line is that getters and setters are a terrible anti-pattern in OOP. Never name your methods like that.

3.6 Don't use "new" outside of secondary ctors

Discuss at `https://goo.gl/U8F8nq`

Let's talk about dependency injection. To be honest, I don't like this name and all the fuzz around it. You know, let's not talk about dependency injection. Instead, we'll talk about clean and disciplined OOP. We will inevitably cover dependency injection, inversion of control, and other "design patterns" related to dependencies.

The problem is not really obvious in small and young applications, but it becomes absolutely crucial and sometimes fatal in bigger systems. Here is an example:

```
class Cash {
  private final int dollars;
  public int euro() {
    return new Exchange().rate("USD", "EUR")
      * this.dollars;
  }
}
```

This is what trouble looks like. We are making an instance of class `Exchange` using operator `new` right inside the method `euro()`. Why is this troublesome? Actually, it is not, as long as the classes are small, simple, and don't use any expensive resources, like network, disk, database, etc.

The troubling name is "hard-coded dependency." Indeed, our class `Cash` is linked to class `Exchange`, and we can't break this dependency without changing the code `inside` class `Cash`.

Imagine a situation where the source code of `Cash` is not

available and we have to use the class anyway. Well, the source code is available but is not modifiable. We just have a library in binary format, and we have to use it. Our code may look like this:

```
Cash five = new Cash("5.00");
print("$5 equals to %d", five.euro());
```

I'm testing method `print()` and don't want to make a round trip to the New York Stock Exchange on every run of my unit test. I don't really care how `five.euro()` works. All I need is the result of it. I don't want to test class `Cash`. I want to test my own code, and I want class `Cash` to stay as quiet as possible during the test run. If it would try to connect to the NYSE over HTTP on every test run, that would be very annoying, and my first question to its developer would be, "Can you please tell me how to configure `Cash` so it will stop talking to the NYSE?"

In the current design of `Cash`, this isn't possible at all. The connection between `Cash` and `Exchange` is *unbreakable*. In order to decouple them, we have to modify the sources of `Cash`. If and when the class is small, this may not be a big problem, but on a larger scale, hard-coded dependencies make our software absolutely untestable and unmaintainable.

The root cause of this problem is operator `new`.

We allow our objects to instantiate other objects when and where they need, so why do we complain when they do this at will? `Cash` is allowed to make an instance of `Exchange`—that's what the problem is. Imagine a situation where the `new` operator is prohibited inside methods. Objects wouldn't be able to create new objects. They would only be allowed to accept them as ctor arguments and encapsulate them in private properties. Class `Cash` would look like this:

```
class Cash {
  private final int dollars;
  private final Exchange exchange;
  Cash(int value, Exchange exch) {
    this.dollars = value;
    this.exchange = exch;
  }
  public int euro() {
    return this.exchange.rate("USD", "EUR")
      * this.dollars;
  }
}
```

The problem is solved. This is how our code will *have* to look:

```
Cash five = new Cash(5, new FakeExchange());
print("$5 equals to %d", five.euro());
```

We have to provide the second argument to the constructor with an instance of `Exchange`. Class `Cash` is not allowed to instantiate it by himself. He can only work with the exchange provided to him. He no longer depends on `Exchange`. Well, he depends, but this dependency is under our control, not his. He doesn't decide where to get the USD-to-EUR rate. He relies on our decision instead, and works with the object we give him.

In other words, instead of letting the object create a dependency he needs, we *inject* it through the constructor.

Such an injection is a good practice. The design of `Cash` so that his ctor expects *all* required dependencies is a very good design. This is how all objects should be designed. For convenience, we may add a few secondary constructors, as explained in Section 1.2:

```
class Cash {
  private final int dollars;
  private final Exchange exchange;
  Cash() { // secondary
    this(0);
  }
  Cash(int value) { // secondary
    this(value, new NYSE());
  }
  Cash(int value, Exchange exch) { // primary
    this.dollars = value;
    this.exchange = exch;
  }
  public int euro() {
    return this.exchange.rate("USD", "EUR")
      * this.dollars;
  }
}
```

When a one-argument constructor is used, an instance of `NYSE` is injected. But this is only a secondary constructor. A primary one allows us to fully control which dependencies our object is working with.

I am suggesting a simple rule that will ensure good design on all your objects: don't use `new` anywhere except in secondary constructors. Look at the code above once again. As you see, operator `new` is used only in one secondary constructor, nowhere else. If you entirely prohibit yourself from using `new` anywhere else, your objects will be fully decoupled from each other, and their testability and maintainability will be much higher.

You may ask what to do when we need an object to instantiate other objects. Let's say we have an object that represents a stream of requests coming from, say, a network socket:

```
class Requests {
  private final Socket socket;
  public Requests(Socket skt) {
    this.socket = skt;
  }
  public Request next() {
    return new SimpleRequest(
      /* read the data from the socket */
    );
  }
}
```

Every call to method `next()` must create a new object of type `Request` and return it. We definitely need an operator `new` here and it's not a ctor. Indeed, this design violates the rule I'm suggesting in this section. This is how we solve it:

```
class Requests {
  private final Socket socket;
  private final Mapping<String, Request> mapping;
  public Requests(Socket skt) {
    this(
      skt,
      new Mapping<String, Request>() {
        @Override
        public Request map(String data) {
          return new SimpleRequest(data);
        }
      }
    );
  }
  public Requests(Socket skt,
    Mapping<String, Request> mpg) {
    this.socket = skt;
    this.mapping = mpg;
  }
  public Request next() {
    return this.mapping.map(
      /* read the data from the socket */
    );
  }
}
```

We encapsulate an instance of `Mapping`, which is responsible for converting our text data into an instance of `Request`. As you see, the `new` operator is used only in the secondary ctor. The method `next()` doesn't have it any more. This design makes class `Requests` very configurable and hard-coded dependency free. There are no more hard-coded dependencies any more. We can inject our own implementation of `Mapping`, which won't use `SimpleRequest`, but will return something else that is more suitable for testing, for example.

It would be great to have such a rule strictly embedded into the language, but that is for the future. In the meantime, keep in mind that every time you use `new` in any method or primary ctor, you're doing something wrong. The only legal place for `new` is in secondary constructors.

I think that is everything you need to know about dependency injection and inversion of control. This one simple rule, in combination with immutable objects, will make your code clean and fully ready for the "injection" of dependencies.

3.7 Avoid type introspection and casting

Discuss at http://goo.gl/BoQ2iq

It is very tempting to occasionally use type introspection and casting, but stay away from both of them at all costs. Technically, I'm talking about the `instanceof` operator and `Class.cast()` method in Java, or their equivalent in other languages. Using this operator, we can check the type of object in runtime. For example:

```
public <T> int size(Iterable<T> items) {
  if (items instanceof Collection) {
    return Collection.class.cast(items).size();
  }
  int size = 0;
  for (T item : items) {
    ++size;
  }
  return size;
}
```

Type introspection is one of the techniques under the umbrella term *reflection*. Reflection is evil too, but it is not directly related to OOP. That's why we won't discuss it in detail. Using reflection, you can modify methods, instructions, statements, classes, objects, types, etc. in runtime. You can simply modify the code before the CPU reaches it. This is a very powerful, and at the same time, very dirty technique that makes your code absolutely unmaintainable. I believe it is just obvious that your code will be very difficult to read if you always have to remember that it is modified by some other code in runtime. It will be a nightmare. In short, I would say that reflection is a great tool... for bad programmers.

This Java method above calculates the size of an iterable. Before going through all of the items, iterating and counting them, it checks whether the object `items` is in reality an instance of `Collection`, where method `size()` already exists. This is an obvious optimization, right? We don't want to iterate them all if we have a faster path. We check the type in runtime and act accordingly.

Even though it looks very convenient and optimal, this is very wrong.

This approach seriously violates the very idea of OOP by *discriminating* objects due to their type. Indeed, according to the type of object `items`, we interact with him differently. Instead of letting the object decide how to perform what's requested, we make a decision apart from him, thereby segregating good objects from bad objects. Philosophically speaking, that is very wrong. It is very disrespectful and offensive. It is very similar to discriminating by gender, ethnicity, or age in the world of humans. When you hire someone to do some work for you, you don't ask for the person's gender. You just tell him or her what needs to be done, and expect the result to satisfy the requirements. Wouldn't it be strange if you said your instructions for a woman were different than the ones for a man? The same applies here for an object. We should avoid discrimination and let them do their job, no matter *who* they are.

Technically speaking, it is also wrong to introspect object types in runtime, because it increases coupling between classes. Look at the example above once again. Our method depends on two interfaces, `Iterable` and `Collection`, instead of just `Iterable`. More dependencies means tighter coupling, which is very bad for maintainability. It is also very bad that these dependencies are hidden. We don't know that the method does this type of introspection internally. The dependency between the method and `Collection` is hidden.

Moreover, in order to use this method in the most effective way, we have to know how it works. We have to check its source code in order to understand that it actually behaves differently if the argument provided is an instance of `Collection`. A much better design would be this one:

```
public <T> int size(Collection<T> items) {
  return items.size();
}
public <T> int size(Iterable<T> items) {
  int size = 0;
  for (T item : items) {
    ++size;
  }
  return size;
}
```

This technique is known as *method overloading* and is not available in all languages. In Ruby, for example, it is not supported, but we can create two methods with different names:

```
def sizeOfIterable(items)
  # ...
end
def sizeOfCollection(items)
  # ...
end
```

Now, the user of the class must make a decision about which method to call. In Java, this decision will be made by compiler, in Ruby, we have to do it manually, having the information about object type in hands.

All this is also true of *class casting*, which is when we force an object to obey a new contract that he has not previously promised to obey:

```
return Collection.class.cast(items).size();
```

This line may also look like this:

```
return ((Collection) items).size();
```

Technically, these two lines operate almost the same. The end result is that object `items` *is a* `Collection`. It is similar to hiring a plumber, but when he enters the house, you say, "I assume you're also a computer specialist; please fix my printer." But wait, here is a more complete example:

```
if (items instanceof Collection) {
    return ((Collection) items).size();
}
```

This sounds like saying, "if you're also a computer specialist, please fix my printer." This sounds much better than just making an assumption and asking him to fix the printer, but it's still very wrong—mostly because of a hidden coupling. Next time, before sending you the plumber, the company will try to select one who is also a computer specialist, because staff will remember that you pay extra for fixing the printer. The contract between you and the plumbing company will still say "fixing the sink", while in reality he is also fixing a printer.

If you decide to change plumbing companies tomorrow, you will have to ask again for someone who can fix your sink and your printer. This knowledge will not be explicitly documented anywhere in your contract. The same problem arises if the company decides to change its staff. Say the guy who was visiting you was fired, so a new person is sent. Your contract is for "fixing a sink." You are given a good plumber, but you are not happy because you're expecting a plumber with some extra skills that are not declared anywhere in the contract.

In other words, you expose your *expectations* for incoming objects without explicitly documenting them. Some clients will *learn* your expectations and provide more suitable objects for you and others won't. Such an unclear, hidden, and implicit relationship between clients and objects will seriously affect maintainability in a negative way.

To summarize, any use of operator `instanceof` or class casting is an anti-pattern and must be avoided. Even though these features are provided by Java and almost all other OOP languages, together with reflection, they do nothing good for your software. They only increase chaos.

Chapter 4

Retirement

An object's lifecycle starts with operator `new` and ends when nobody needs him anymore. Usually, objects do their work and we don't complain. Sometimes, though, they throw exceptions when they are not happy about the situation they see. Exceptions are a great technique in OOP that actually have nothing to do with the object paradigm, but they help tremendously in error handling and code optimization. Thanks to exceptions, we don't need to worry about how to handle problems in every single method. We can just escalate them all to a higher level. We'll discuss what to do with them there a bit later.

However, exceptions are easy to use incorrectly. Very incorrectly. And there is nothing worse for maintainability than incorrect error handling.

This chapter is about `NULL` as a result of methods, exception handling, and resource acquisition. The content is rather controversial and not very practical, yet. By "yet", I mean the current situation with object-oriented languages. I really hope that in the near future, some of the ideas in this chapter will be implemented in new or existing OOP languages.

4.1 Never return NULL

Discuss at http://goo.gl/TzrYbz

`NULL`, as a method argument, is a bad thing, as we already discussed in Sections 3.3 and 2.6.5. A very bad thing. I'm not sure about other programming styles, but in object-oriented and procedural, for sure. Now let's discuss why returning `NULL` is also a terrible idea. As usual, let's start with a Java example:

```
public String title() {
  if (/* no title here */) {
    return null;
  }
  return "Elegant Objects";
}
```

It is so ugly, and at the same time, so common that I don't even know where to start. Let's begin with why it is ugly, and then we will try to analyze why it is very common in the object-oriented world.

First of all, this design encourages us to do exactly what Section 3.3 argues against: treat objects as handicapped creatures. We simply can't trust the object returned by `title()`. We can't trust his abilities. He is disabled. He needs special treatment:

```
String title = x.title();
print(title.length());
```

We can't call `title.length()` without being afraid of hitting a `NullPointerException`. And the problem is not in the exception itself. The exception is just a technical inconvenience. The problem is bigger. The problem is that our *trust* is lost. We simply can't say that our objects are self-sufficient, solid, respectable, smart, etc. They are not. We can't just tell them what to do and rely on the result. We have to check whether the object is the object in the first place. This check is a terrible violation of the object-oriented paradigm:

```
String title = x.title();
if (title == null) {
  print("Can't print; it's not a title.");
  return;
}
print(title.length());
```

The idea of an object is that it is an entity we *trust*. It is not a piece of data that doesn't know anything about our intentions and simply provides some space in memory with convenient access to it and a few convenient sub-routines. It is not a token we send from one place to another. It is not an envelope for the data. No, it is not.

An object is a living organism, with his own lifecycle, his own behavior, and his own state. He either exists and is alive, or he doesn't exist and is dead. There is no third state. A *variable* is just a nickname for an object.

```
String t = x.title();
```

Here, `t` is just a nickname for the object returned by method `title()`. We trust our object, and we trust the variable that means exactly the same as the object. By trust, I mean that the object is fully *responsible* for his own actions and we are not going to interfere in any way. However he wants to work is how he will work. If he wants to print the name, we will accept that. If he wants to throw an exception instead, that's fine for us too. But we won't throw an exception without even talking to him!

This is absolutely wrong and *disrespectful*:

```
if (title == null) {
  print("Can't print; it's not a title.");
  return;
}
```

This check is an obvious sign of a lack of trust in the application. I don't trust `title()`, and someone else will eventually not trust me. Use of `NULL` will lead to a big loss of trust in the entire software and will turn it into an unmaintainable mess. Yes, this is also about *maintainability*. A lack of trust leads to a serious loss of maintainability simply because when I read the code, I need more time to understand which method call I can trust and which one can return `NULL`. I also have to double check this result before actually using it and talking to the returned object.

It is very similar to a working relationship in a team. If every time my coworker gives me a new document, I have to double check whether he cheated or made everything right, our work will seriously slow down. Don't get me wrong, I'm not against quality control. We do have to check whether our output is valid and we do have to double check, but someone else has to be responsible for that, not me, the recipient of a document from my coworker. I have to get the document and immediately start working with it. I have to be able to *trust* my coworker. And this is not about a personal relationship, but the speed of work within the entire team. We *need* trust, yet `NULL` is taking it away from us.

If my coworkers are able to cheat and return `NULL`, my work will slow down significantly. I will have to check all of them and my code will become much more verbose. I will easily forget to check sooner or later. I won't feel safe on my own team, in my own software.

To summarize, it is just wrong and ugly. A method that returns `NULL` is disrespectful. It doesn't respect me as its user because it cheats and returns a broken document to me.

But why is it so common and popular? Look at method `listFiles()` in class `Files` of Java 1.2. It is supposed to list all files in the directory and return an array of them. It doesn't throw an exception if there is no directory and returns `NULL` instead. This is how I'm supposed to use it:

```
void list(File dir) {
  File[] files = dir.listFiles();
  if (files == null) {
    throw new IOException("Directory is absent.");
  }
  for (File file : files) {
    System.out.println(file.getName());
  }
}
```

This is how I would use it if it threw an exception instead of returning `NULL`:

```
void list(File dir) {
  for (File file : dir.listFiles()) {
    System.out.println(file.getName());
  }
}
```

I think it's obvious that the second snippet is shorter, cleaner, more maintainable, and just better. Why did Java designers decide to return `NULL` instead of throwing `IOException`? I think they hadn't heard of the *fail fast* principle at the time they designed the JDK. They thought it was better to quietly return `NULL` and let me throw an exception if necessary instead of throwing one right after realizing that the directory is actually absent. They were trying to do us a favor, but they didn't at all.

4.1.1 Fail fast vs. fail safe

There are basically two opposite philosophies regarding software robustness and failure resilience: fail *fast* or fail *safe*. I am a big fan of the first, and strongly against the second.

Fail safe basically motivates us to do as much as possible to keep the software running, even when we hit a bug, an input/output problem, a memory overflow, etc. No matter what happens, the software should try to survive. Returning `NULL` is a survival technique. For example, if we see that a directory is absent while we're asked to list all the files in it, can we list them? No, we can't. Obviously, the request is invalid. Its author didn't check the directory before asking us to list the files in it. It's his or her fault, but we will try to *save* the situation. We won't throw `IOException`. Instead, we will return `NULL` to let someone handle this situation somehow. Hopefully, no one will try to iterate the array returned, and it won't hit a `NullPointerException`. Hopefully.

Fail fast is the opposite approach. It motivates us to stop execution and throw an exception as soon as we see a problem—any problem. We should not worry about the consequences. We should make our software as fragile as possible and then cover it with unit tests. If it is fragile and breaks at every single control point, unit tests will easily reproduce these situations and we'll fix them. If it breaks in production, we can easily add a test that reproduces this situation, simply because all breaking points are obvious and well-documented. We emphasize them instead of hiding them. We make them visible and easy to trace. We throw `IOException` right at the moment we find out the directory is absent. We are not going to save the situation. Instead, we're going to make it as *flagrant* as possible. If they gave us an invalid directory location, let them pay for this mistake. They will have to fix the bug on their side and be more careful next time.

Which approach is better? As I said, I am a big fan of fail fast. I think that stability and robustness can only be achieved if errors are revealed and immediately reported. The sooner we find the problem and the faster we crash, the better the overall quality will eventually be. To the contrary, the longer we conceal the problem, the bigger the trouble will become.

This may sound counter intuitive because we don't want to stop our software. We don't want it to crash. We don't want to see the stack traces. And that's a trap. We don't want to face the fact that our software has bugs. Actually, it is full of bugs. Some of them are obvious and visible while others are properly hidden. But they are there. By hiding that fact, we are doing ourselves a bad favor. Instead of revealing the wound and curing it, we're hiding it and lying to our patient that everything will be fine. The sooner we see the problems, the sooner we fix them. The faster they surface, the faster our response will be. And every bug fix will make our product more stable and robust.

Why do so many Java methods return `NULL` instead of throwing exceptions? Most probably because they believe in the fail safe philosophy. I don't. And I highly recommend you stay away from it too. Fail fast is the way to go if you care about the quality of the entire application, not just a single method.

4.1.2 Alternatives to NULL

What are the alternatives to returning `NULL`? Sometimes it is very tempting to return `NULL` when the object we're looking for can't be found. For example:

```
public User user(String name) {
  if (/* not found in database */) {
    return null;
  }
  return /* from database */;
}
```

In my experience, this is the most common case where `NULL` is returned instead of a real object. We simply can't find a better way to tell our clients, "the object you're looking for doesn't exist." We don't want to throw an exception, because we don't see this situation as being exceptional. The client is looking for a user in the database, but the user is not there. We don't want the entire application to crash in this situation, right? It is a pretty standard and routine situation. The user is not found, so we return `NULL` and move on.

As you understand, this thinking is very close to the "fail safe" philosophy explained above. Don't do this. Instead, there are a few alternatives to `NULL`.

The first option is to split the method into two methods. The first method will check for the existence of an object, and the second one will return it. The second one will throw an exception if nothing is found:

```
public boolean exists(String name) {
  if (/* not found in database */) {
    return false;
  }
  return true;
}
public User user(String name) {
  return /* from database */;
}
```

The problem with this approach is obvious: It is ineffective. We will make a roundtrip to the database two times. First, we will check for the existence of a record in the database, then we will go there again to fetch the object.

That's why there is a second option. Instead of returning `NULL` or throwing an exception, we can return a collection of objects. For example:

```
public Collection<User> users(String name) {
  if (/* not found in database */) {
    return new ArrayList<>(0);
  }
  return Collections.singleton(
    /* from database */
  );
}
```

If nothing is found, the collection will be empty. The client will have to work through it somehow to retrieve objects. Technically, this is not very different from `NULL`, but a bit cleaner. Pay attention that I renamed the method. It is now called `users()` instead of `user()`.

Yet another option is to use class `java.util.Optional` (in Java 8) or something similar. It is the same as the collection, but may contain only one element. I find this solution counter-OOP and would not recommend you use it, mostly because it is semantically incorrect. The method name will still be `user()`, while the returned object is not really a user but rather some sort of an envelope around a user. It's misleading and not in the spirit of object thinking. It is very close to a `NULL` reference. Don't use it.

The last option I'm aware of is a null object design pattern—when nothing is found, we return an object that looks like a normal one, but behaves differently. He does something, but he doesn't do something else. For example, when we're looking for a user by the name `"Jeff"` and he is not found, we return an object that has this name and return it if anyone asks him via `name()`. But on all other requests, he throws exceptions. This approach truly aligns with the spirit of object thinking, but can be used in limited situations. Pay attention that the type of the returned object stays the same. An instance of `NullUser` is an object of the same type as a regular `SqlUser`, for example. They both implement the same interface `User`. For example, this is how `NullUser` may look:

```
class NullUser implements User {
  private final String label;
  NullUser(String name) {
    this.label = name;
  }
  @Override
  public String name() {
    return this.label;
  }
  @Override
  public void raise(Cash salary) {
    throw new IllegalStateException(
      "You can't raise my salary, I'm a stub"
    );
  }
}
```

To summarize, never return NULL . Never even think about it. There are no excuses for the existence of NULL in OOP. It is a toxic keyword in Java and other languages. Just stay away from it. When you need to return something that is not found, either throw an exception, return a collection, or return a null object. These are the three best alternatives.

4.2 Throw only checked exceptions

Discuss at http://goo.gl/5tGDEc

It is time to talk about checked and unchecked exceptions. Even though most object-oriented languages have only unchecked ones, Java has them both. Let me summarize the content of this section upfront: unchecked exceptions are a mistake, and all exceptions must be checked. Moreover, multiple exception types are a bad idea too.

This attitude is rather abstract and impractical, because it goes strongly against the current situation in most programming platforms. In most of them, including Ruby, C#, Python, Scala, and many others, unchecked exceptions are the only instrument available. They simply don't have checked exceptions. That's why almost everything I say in this section can probably change your way of thinking, but it won't give you any real, practical recommendations unless you're writing in Java or planning to create your own object-oriented language.

However, I hope that future OOP languages will be much stricter than existing ones and will pay more attention to error handling through exceptions. What I'm proposing below is, I believe, the right way of managing exceptions. It is more logical and clean. I will demonstrate it now.

First, let's see what the difference between checked and unchecked is and what exception "types" are used for. This is how a checked exception situation looks in Java:

```
public byte[] content(File file) throws IOException {
  byte[] array = new byte[1000];
  new FileInputStream(file).read(array);
  return array;
}
```

Pay attention to the signature of this simple method, as it ends with `throws IOException`. This means that when I call `content()`, I have to catch that exception no matter what:

```
public int length(File file) {
  try {
    return content(file).length();
  } catch (IOException ex) {
    // I have to do something about this
    // exception and either resolve
    // it right here or escalate it to a higher
    // level.
  }
}
```

I can't just call method `content()` without being fully responsible for a problem it may cause. By "problem" I mean an `IOException`. This method is not really "safe" as it may cause trouble. I mean an `IOException` again. It may crash because of some problem with the input/output system. I assume the crash is going to be related to the file system. By saying `throws IOException`, the method basically transfers *responsibility* to my shoulders. It is making it my decision for what to do when there is some trouble with the file.

I can also do the same by *escalating* the responsibility to my clients and declaring myself "unsafe" as well:

```
public int length(File file) throws IOException {
  return content(file).length();
}
```

In this example, I don't catch the exception anymore. I let it "float" up. I escalate the problem, like we do in management. Higher levels in the hierarchy of calls will have to do something about it, not me. I'm simply saying that I don't know what to do with this situation, so please help me.

Exception type `IOException` is "checked", because it has to be caught. We can't just ignore its existence in the method `length()`. We have to either `catch` or declare ourselves as `throws IOException`. That's why checked exceptions are always *visible*. While working with method `length()`, we have to remember that we're dealing with a *toxic* and *unsafe* method called `content()`. We should either declare ourselves unsafe as well, or remove the toxicity by catching and resolving it somehow.

To the contrary, "unchecked" exceptions can be ignored and never caught. If and when they occur, they automatically float up until someone catches them. But the language doesn't mandate that we do anything about them. For example, exception type `IllegalArgumentException` is "unchecked":

```
public int length(File file) throws IOException {
  if (!file.exists()) {
    throw new IllegalArgumentException(
      "File doesn't exist; I can't count its length."
    );
  }
  return content(file).length();
}
```

In this example, the method signature doesn't say anything about

`IllegalArgumentException`. When someone calls `length()`, he or she will not know what to expect. The information about `IllegalArgumentException` is hidden. That's what I meant when I said before that checked exceptions are always *visible*.

4.2.1 Don't catch unless you have to

It is an obvious choice we have to make when designing a method—to catch all exceptions here and now, making the method look "safe" for its users, or escalate problems. I am in favor of the second option. Escalate them all as much as you can. Every `catch` statement has to have a very strong reason for its existence. In other words, don't catch unless you really have to do it, and there is no other choice.

In an ideal design, there has to be only one `catch` statement per point of entrance into the application. For example, if it is a mobile app communicating with the user through the phone screen, it has a single entrance and must have a single `catch` in the entire application. Unfortunately, that is very rarely possible, mostly because Java itself and many existing frameworks are designed with a different idea in mind.

We already discussed the difference between Fail Fast and Fail Safe in Section 4.1.1. The same applies here, almost literally. The philosophy of making the software robust by solving problems right where they occur and at all costs makes the entire code unmaintainable and very unstable. This is how we can do it in our method:

```
public int length(File file) {
  try {
    return content(file).length();
  } catch (IOException ex) {
    return 0;
  }
}
```

Method `length()` is perfectly safe now. No matter what happens with the file system, it doesn't crash. It returns an integer and the entire application will continue to run. It is a typical example of a Fail Safe approach. We see a problem, but we don't want to upset our client. We want to look nice and never crash. We want to be reliable. That's why we return zero, when in reality the file system is, for example, running out of file handlers. The file system can't return the file length, even though the file exists. It signals us, it screams, and it cries, but we ignore it. No matter what is happening, we hide this information. We simply return zero.

Needless to say, by hiding a problem, we're doing a very bad service to everyone, including the client calling method `length()`. Yes, the application won't crash right now because it will obtain a zero and will continue to do something else. But eventually it will crash, because that zero is not the right file length. It will crash far away from the call to `length()`, and it won't be possible to understand what caused the crash. It will take hours of debugging to find out that the number returned by `length()` was actually an indicator of a mistake in the file system.

This approach is also known as "using exceptions for flow control." Indeed, in the example above, we are using a signal about an exception in order to fork execution. We're doing something like this, but with the help of exceptions:

```
public int length(File file) {
  if (/* There is a problem in the file system. */)
    return 0;
  } else {
    return content(file).length();
  }
}
```

This is a legal way of forking, but exceptions are not the right tool for that. Exceptions are not designed to help us fork. Instead, they are supposed to indicate a critical and non-recoverable situation that causes a full termination of the normal flow of operations and takes some extraordinary measures. We'll talk more about *recoverability* in a few minutes.

Some may argue that instead of returning zero as a file size, we may return `-1` or `NULL`. We already discussed why returning `NULL` is a terrible idea in Section 4.1. Returning `-1` is not really much different than that, because it is not a null object, but a scalar value, which is semantically very close to `NULL`. Well, almost identical. OK, not almost; it's absolutely identical. By returning `-1`, we're forcing our clients to not trust the result returned and always double check it:

```
int length = length(new File("test.txt"));
if (length == -1) {
  print("Hm ... there is something wrong.");
} else {
  print("File size is %d" + length);
}
```

This comparison, using the operator `==`, is the problem. This is a sign of mistrust involving the object `length`, as we already discussed in Section 4.1. We do expect a file length, but we get something else. It is not a length, but a signal for us that we should not treat it as a number. We need to remember that such a "betrayal" may happen, and we should be ready for it. If we forget to compare using `==`, we may end up in serious trouble. For example, we will start reading `length` bytes from the file, while `length` is actually `-1`. The consequences will be unpredictable. And, more importantly, it will be very difficult to detect the cause of the problem.

My point is that catching an exception and "rescuing" the situation is a very serious action that has to have a very good cause. Every time you rescue without rethrowing, you're putting yourself in a Fail Safe mindset.

By the way, do I have to mention that "catching and logging" is a terrible anti-pattern? I believe it's just obvious already.

4.2.2 Always chain exceptions

Wait, we didn't discuss what "rethrowing" is. This is how it looks, and it is a perfectly valid practice:

```
public int length(File file) throws Exception {
  try {
    return content(file).length();
  } catch (IOException ex) {
    throw new Exception(
      "Can't calculate file length.",
      ex
    );
  }
}
```

I catch the exception here, but I immediately throw a new one. It is a good practice to use "exception chaining", just like I did here.

I'm not ignoring the fact that a problem occurred by replacing it with a new one. Instead, I'm wrapping the original problem into a new one and throwing them up together.

If this chaining happens many times, the exception that floats up will look like a soap bubble with a bubble inside it. That bubble will also contain a bubble, etc. There will be many layers. The `catch` statement that finally decides to do something about the problem and rescue the situation will burst the bubble and take all other bubbles out of it. How that `catch` will handle the situation and report the problem to the user doesn't really matter. What is important is that we bring the low-level root cause of the problem to the highest level of the entire software.

The code below, though, would be a bad idea, because it ignores the root cause.

```
public int length(File file) throws Exception {
  try {
    return content(file).length();
  } catch (IOException ex) {
    // Here I ignore the problem, 'ex', and create
    // a new one, of a new type, with a new
    // message:
    throw new Exception("Can't calculate it");
  }
}
```

This is a very bad practice indeed. We lose very valuable information about the root cause of the problematic input/output situation. That object `ex` probably had a message inside it, probably something like `"Too many open files (24)"`. We ignore it and create a new exception that says `"Can't calculate it"`. This new exception will float up and be caught eventually by a `catch` statement on the top level of the application. Very valuable low-level information will be lost. It will take hours or days to find out why exactly the length of the file wasn't able to be calculated.

I'm sure this is just obvious, but let me reiterate anyway: always chain exceptions, and never ignore original ones.

But why do we need exception chaining in the first place, you may ask. Why can't we just let exceptions float up and declare all our methods unsafe? In the example above, why catch `IOException` and throw it again, "wrapped" into `Exception`? What is wrong with the existing `IOException`? The answer is obvious: exception chaining semantically enriches the problem context. In other words, just receiving `"Too many open files (24)"` is not enough. It is too low-level. Instead, we want to see a chain of exceptions where the original one says that there are too many open files, the next one says that the file length can't be calculated, the next one claims that the content of the image can't be read, etc. If a user can't open his or her own profile picture, just returning "too many files" is not enough.

Ideally, each method has to catch all exceptions possible and rethrow them through chaining. Once again, catch everything, chain, and immediately rethrow. This is the best approach to exception handling.

4.2.3 Recover only once

There is a very popular concept of "recovering" after an exception that we have to discuss. Actually, we just discussed it a few pages ago. It is the same conflict between Fail Fast and Fail Safe, but from a different angle. I'm saying we can't "recover" after an exception if we are in Fail Fast territory. Simply put, there is no such thing as recovery. It is just another name for an already known anti-pattern, which is "using exceptions for flow control." This is what you may know as recovery after an exception:

```
int age;
try {
  age = Integer.parseInt(text);
} catch (NumberFormatException ex) {
  // This is where we "recover" after the exception.
  age = -1;
}
```

How is it different than the examples we discussed above? There is no difference at all. It is just an anti-pattern, very similar to returning `NULL`, which we explained in Section 4.1.

But I'm not entirely right. We do have to recover, once. We have to let all our methods throw exceptions and never catch them, as discussed in the previous section. All exceptions will then float up to the highest point of the application. To a few points, actually. I mean entry points, where a user communicates with the application. For example, if it is a command line tool that is supposed to be executed by a user through a terminal, the code will look like this:

```
public class App {
  public static void main(String... args) {
    try {
      System.out.println(new App().run());
    } catch (Exception ex) {
      System.err.println(
        "I'm sorry, there was a problem:"
        + ex.getLocalizedMessage()
      );
    }
  }
}
```

As you see, I don't rethrow anything inside this `catch` statement. I solve the problem here and now. I just show the problem to the user, and that's it. My static method `main` is not toxic. It is safe. It never crashes, because it is the highest level of the application. There is nothing on top of it.

If I don't catch the problem here, it will float up to the runtime environment, and Java Virtual Machine will catch it anyway. If this happens, the user will also see a message, but it won't be friendly at all. It will be a system message, exposing the entire stack trace to the user. I don't want that to happen. Instead, I want to "recover."

This is the only legal place for recovery.

The same should happen at every entrance point. There are not so many of them, even in complex systems. What I'm saying is that there are just a few legal places for recovering in any software. Everywhere else, we must catch and rethrow or not catch at all. The first option is preferable. Always catch, chain, and rethrow. Recover only once at the highest level. That's it.

4.2.4 Use aspect-oriented programming

Sometimes we need to retry an operation when it fails. Say we're trying to download a web page via an HTTP request. It is very possible that a network connection will fail once in a while. It would be sad to show a failure message to a user and ask him or her to rerun the application. We can retry ourselves, right? But in order to retry, we have to catch an exception and recover:

```
public String content() throws IOException {
  int attempt = 0;
  while (true) {
    try {
      return http();
    } catch (IOException ex) {
      if (attempt >= 2) {
        throw ex;
      }
    }
  }
}
```

This method will make three attempts, at most, before failing with `IOException`. This method is unsafe, but it's "not immediately" unsafe. It makes a few attempts before escalating the problem. Even though it's a very practical design, it contradicts everything said above in this section, because it does recover before the highest level. Bad practice? Yes. Is there a better solution? Not really.

Well, yes, there is one: aspect-oriented programming (AOP). It is a very simple, yet very powerful programming paradigm that fits extremely well into the OOP world. It is not really a paradigm, but a basic technique that can seriously simplify typical operations and take away verbosity from OOP code. Indeed, look at the code above once again. It is very verbose as it is. It takes 10 lines just to retry a single method call. And it is still very primitive. A proper implementation would be much longer. In a properly implemented retrying mechanism, we would not ignore the exception, but would log it somehow. We would also add some delay between attempts, which would grow algorithmically. Also, we would make the number of attempts configurable instead of being a hard-coded constant 3. Using AOP on top of Java 6, we would do it like this:

```
@RetryOnFailure(attempts = 3)
public String content() throws IOException {
    return http();
}
```

This annotation, `@RetryOnFailure`, will be picked up at compile time and "wrap" method `content()` in a "retry on failure" code block[1]. This code block is called an "aspect." Technically, it is an object that receives control and decides how and when to call `content()`. It is sort of an adapter in front of `content()`. The beauty of AOP is that we avoid code duplication by moving supplementary techniques and mechanisms away from our main classes. I would highly recommend you read more about AOP and use it in your projects, no matter what language you're writing in.

AOP is mentioned here just to demonstrate that premature recovering after exceptions in OOP is indeed a bad practice that can be replaced by another technique. Retrying on failure is one of the examples where AOP helps us stay clean in OOP while being practical and pragmatic.

---

[1]You can see this annotation and its AOP aspect in action here: `http://aspects.jcabi.com/`

4.2.5 Just one exception type is enough

If you agree with the "never recover" and "always chain" principles explained above, you would understand why exception typing is a redundant feature. Indeed, if we recover only once, we have an exception object that contains all other exceptions inside it when that happens. Properly chained, why do we need to know its type?

Moreover, we never use exceptions for flow control, right? We never catch exceptions in order to decide what to do next. We only catch in order to rethrow, right? If that's the case, we don't really care about the type of exception we're catching. We will rethrow it anyway. We simply don't need this information, because we never use it. We don't catch exceptions on their way up. Even when we do catch, we do it for only one purpose: to chain them and rethrow.

4.3 Be either final or abstract

Discuss at http://goo.gl/vo9F2g

I haven't said anything about *inheritance* yet. Now it's time to talk about this very powerful, and very often abused, feature of OOP. I frequently hear people saying that inheritance is just evil and must be avoided. They say that encapsulation is a better alternative in most cases. I think I agree with them, but let's analyze why inheritance causes problems and what can be done to prevent them. Indeed, we don't want to entirely get rid of inheritance, but we do want to use it right.

The strongest argument against inheritance is that it makes relations between objects too complex. It is simply very difficult to understand a hierarchy of classes that inherit each other when the height of such a pyramid is, say, five levels or more. This makes total sense, but the root cause of the problem is not inheritance by itself. *Virtual methods* cause the problem. Let's look at this example:

```
class Document {
  public int length() {
    return this.content().length();
  }
  public byte[] content() {
    // Loads the raw content of the
    // document as an array of bytes.
  }
}
```

It's not a perfect design for a document abstraction, but it is good enough to demonstrate how inheritance may cause problems for code readability. Let's try to extend this class to enable the loading of an encrypted document:

```
class EncryptedDocument extends Document {
  @Override
  public byte[] content() {
    // Loads the document, decrypts it on the fly,
    // and returns the decrypted content.
  }
}
```

It looks valid, right? Method `content()` in class `EncryptedDocument` loads the content and decrypts it on the fly. But the behavior of method `length()`, which is inherited by `EncryptedDocument` from `Document`, is changed. It doesn't return the length of the document on disk anymore. It returns the length of the decoded content instead. Is it what we would expect it to do? Not necessarily. We would probably expect it to return the length of the physical storage consumed by the document, like it works in class `Document`.

Will it be easy to understand what is wrong with method `length()` in the child class `EncryptedDocument`? It will take some time. We will have to remember that it calls method `content()`, which was overriden. We will be looking at the source code of class `Document` because the method `length()` is there, keeping in mind that some of the methods it is calling are located in child classes. This type of thinking is rather counterintuitive. Inheritance, intuitively, is a top-down process, where child classes inherit code from parent classes. Method overriding makes it possible for a parent class to access the code of a child class. Such reverse thinking goes against common sense, so to speak.

This is where inheritance from a convenient OOP instrument

turns into a maintainability problem. Complexity grows, and the code becomes very difficult to read and understand. However, there is a solution. Just make your classes and methods either `final` or `abstract`, and the very possibility of a problem fades away. Indeed, if class `Document` would be `final`, we would not be able to extend it in the first place. On the other hand, if its method `content()` would be `abstract`, we would not be able to implement it in `Document`, and `length()` would not be confused.

There are basically three possible statuses of a class: he can be either `final`, `abstract`, or neither. A `final` class is a "black box" for his users. He can't be modified by inheritance. He is solid and self-sufficient. He knows how to work, and doesn't need any help. We technically can't override any methods in a `final` class. They are final forever.

An `abstract` class is a "glass box", which is incomplete. He can't work by himself, he needs help, and he has missing components. He is not a class yet, technically speaking. He is raw material that can be used to create a proper class. Technically, we can override certain methods in an `abstract` class, while others are `final`.

The third state, which is neither `final` nor `abstract`, is what I'm strongly against, because it is neither a black nor a glass box. It is rather confusing, because it may become either one. We can override some of its methods, thus treating the class as a glass box. However, at the same time, the class may think of itself as a black box. The class will assume that it is solid, self-sufficient, and robust, while someone is allowed to violate this assumption and replace certain elements of it through virtual methods.

This is how the design of `Document` would look if Java would not allow me to create classes and methods that are neither `final` nor `abstract`:

```
final class Document {
  public int length() { /* the same */ }
  public byte[] content() { /* the same */ }
}
```

Pay attention to the `final` modifier. It tells the compiler that none of the methods in this class can be overridden by its children. Now, we have to create an `EncryptedDocument`. It has to be a `Document`, but we can't extend it. Thus, we have to introduce an interface, which is a very good practice as already mentioned in Section 2.3:

```
interface Document {
  int length();
  byte[] content();
}
```

Then we have to rename our `Document` to something like `DefaultDocument`, and make sure it implements interface `Document`:

```
final class DefaultDocument implements Document {
  @Override
  public int length() { /* the same */ }
  @Override
  public byte[] content() { /* the same */ }
}
```

Now the last step: We need to create `EncryptedDocument`, reusing the functionality of `DefaultDocument`. We will use encapsulation instead of inheritance, because inheritance is just not possible for a `final` class:

```
final class EncryptedDocument implements Document {
  private final Document plain;
  EncryptedDocument(Document doc) {
    this.plain = doc;
  }
  @Override
  public int length() {
    return this.plain.length();
  }
  @Override
  public byte[] content() {
    byte[] raw = this.plain.content();
    return /* Decrypt the raw content. */;
  }
}
```

Pay attention to the fact that both classes `DefaultDocument` and `EncryptedDocument` are `final` and can't be extended.

This example illustrates that inheritance won't be possible in most places, due to the mandatory use of `final` and `abstract`. If all classes are `final`, only encapsulation will be available.

If you follow this principle and make all your classes `final` or `abstract`, you will almost never use inheritance. But sometimes you will, when it makes sense. When does it make sense? Only when you need to *refine* class behavior, not extend, but refine. There is a difference. Extending means that an existing behavior is partially supplemented by a new one. Refining means that partially incomplete behavior is made complete.

We should not be able to "extend" anything in OOP, because this process, as I demonstrated above, treats objects as glass boxes when they don't want that. They are designed to be treated as black boxes and do not expect us to intrude and violate their solidarity. Extending a class is an intrusion.

Instead, we should only *refine* `abstract` classes, which expect us to do that. For example, we may have a `Document` that is incomplete but knows how to calculate its length:

```
abstract class Document {
  public abstract byte[] content();
  public final int length() {
    return this.content().length;
  }
}
```

Now, we will have to *refine* it by introducing a new class, `DefaultDocument`, which knows how to load the content from, say, a disk:

```
final class DefaultDocument extends Document {
  @Override
  public byte[] content() {
    // Loads the content from disk.
  }
}
```

Then we create class `EncryptedDocument`, which refines `Document` differently:

```
final class EncryptedDocument extends Document {
  @Override
  public byte[] content() {
    // Loads the content from disk,
    // decrypts it, and returns it.
  }
}
```

You may say that in this design, we have the same problem as above: method `length()` will return the size of a decrypted document instead of a real file on disk. Yes, that's true, but it's done consciously. Both classes are refining an `abstract` class, clearly seeing how method `length()` is using their own methods. That's why refinement is a much cleaner approach than extension.

To summarize, the ability to make classes and methods neither `final` nor `abstract` is an evil feature in Java and many other languages. We have to be explicit in our intentions—either a method is designed the right way, or it is not designed at all. There is nothing in between.

4.4 Use RAII

Discuss at https://goo.gl/ULUJ8o

Resource Acquisition Is Initialization (RAII) is the last thing I want to mention before we finish. It is a very powerful technique that exists in C++ but is missing in Java, simply because Java destroys objects through garbage collection. That's why it doesn't have destructors. Of course, we can emulate RAII in Java, but C++ does it in a much nicer fashion. Let's see how it works in C++. Imagine that we have a text file abstraction:

```
#include <stdio.h>
#include <string>
class Text {
public:
  Text(const char* name) {
    this->f = fopen(name, "r");
  }
  ~Text() {
    fclose(this->f);
  }
  const std::string& content() {
    // Reads file content and returns
    // it back as a UTF-8 string.
  }
private:
  FILE* f;
};
```

Here is how we would use this class:

```
int main() {
  Text t("/tmp/test.txt");
  t->content();
}
```

First, we create `t`, an object of class `Text`, calling its constructor `Text()`. Then we call method `content()` to read the file. Then we exit the scope of visibility of object `t` and destructor `~Text()` is called. The destructor closes the file.

The trick is that the resource is captured while an object is alive. In this example, a file handle `f` will be captured until a destructor is called. That's where the name of this technique comes from—resource acquisition is initialization. We acquire a resource when an object is initialized. We release the resource when the object is no longer required and is destroyed. The technique is very convenient. I highly advise that you use it whenever possible.

In Java and many other high-level languages, this RAII technique is not applicable, simply because they don't have destructors. In Java, for example, objects are being destroyed in the background when they are not used anymore. This process is called *garbage collection*. Technically, this means that in Java, object `t` would still be alive even after method `main()` finishes its execution. Do we need that object after the end of method `main()`? No, but Java doesn't destroy it immediately. Instead, it lets it stay in memory for a long time and calls it "garbage." Only when there is not enough memory for new objects does the garbage collector remove the object.

That's why there are no destructors in Java. Unfortunately.

However, we can do something similar to RAII in Java 7 too. We can use `try with resource`:

```
int main() {
  try (Text t = new Text("/tmp/test.txt")) {
    t.content();
  }
}
```

Object `t` will not be destroyed by the end of the `try` block, but its method `close()` will be called, which is very close to the idea of a destructor in C++. We just need to make sure our class `Text` implements the `Closeable` interface.

I highly recommend that you use RAII everywhere you work with real resources, like files, streams, database connections, etc. In C++, use destructors, and in Java, use `AutoCloseable`.

Epilogue

I strongly believe that the future of object-oriented programming is bright. Java, C#, C++, Ruby, Python, and other *pseudo*-OOP languages will be replaced by ones that are stricter, cleaner, and more elegant. I don't know when this will happen, but I have no doubt that it will.

The problem is not really in the lack of good languages. The problem is in us, in our mindset, in our understanding of OOP, in the way we think and design our software, and in our mentality and principles. We have to change the way we code, and the software will respond gratefully. The languages will start to change when we start to use them differently.

I want us to change our way of thinking. That is why I wrote this book.

The end.
California, Malta, Ukraine
2015-2016

Designed in LaTeX

Index

`==`, 43, 145, 186, 200
`NULL`, **86**, 144, 185, 192, 200
`NullPointerException`, 86, 150, 185
`abstract`, 211
`calloc()`, 160
`delete`, 19
`equals()`, 43, 155
`final`, 211
`for`, 142
`free()`, 160
`hashCode()`, 155
`if`, 17, 141, 142
`instanceof`, 178
`malloc()`, 160
`new`, 19, 20, 46, 171, 174, 177
`static`, 64
`struct`, 163
`switch`, 142
`while`, 142

abstraction, 120
adjective, 62
aggregation, 43
algorithm, 46
Android, 92
anthropomorphization, 22, 50, 56
Assembly, 119

Beck, Kent, 95
behavior, 46, 153
Bloch, Joshua, 80
boolean, 61
builder, 53

C, 25, 56, 119, 137, 146–148
C++, 19, 36, 159, 163
caching, 38
class, **19**, 46
    abstract, 213
    micro, 142
class casting, 180
Clojure, 138
code duplication, 32, 65
cohesion, 68, 115, 129
complexity, 42
composition, 35
computer thinking, 121
constant, 64, 151
constructor, 27, **33**, 35, 165, 173
    primary, 29, 173
    private, 132
    secondary, 29, 174
contract, 70
coordinates, 44, 153
coupling, 52, 66, 127, 172
    temporal, **83**, 129

221

data, 43, 68, 113, 151, 162
    naked, 166
data structure, 164
declarative style, **122**, 140, 166
decorator, 38
    composable, 140
decoupling, 50
dependency, 67, 136, 173
    Dependency Injection, 171
destructor, 216
discrimination, 179
documentation, 94

encapsulation, 33, 35, **42**, 42, 46, 166
equality, 43
exception, 195
    chaining, 201
exclusive lock, 89
execution, 46
expressiveness, 128

factory, 19, 132
Factory Pattern, 19, 20
fail fast, 188, **189**, 198
fakes, **98**
Feathers, Michael, 96
flexibility, 28, 37
Freeman, Steve, 97

garbage collection, 216, 217
getter, 55, 162
Goetz, Brian, 77
Groovy, 129

Haskell, 138
helper, 132

IDE, 168
identity, 42, 44, 79, 153
immutability, **74**, 74–76, 79–81, 83–85, 151, 177
imperative style, **122**, 147, 166

inheritance, 87, **209**
initialization, **28**, 33, 37, 83, 84, 165
input/output, 151
instance, 19, 35
instantiation, 34, **35**, 38, 46, 83, 84
interface, 35, **50**, 50, 99, 104, 107

Java, 19, 22, 27–29, 33, 34, 36, 38, 42, 47, 48, 50, 60, 64, 66, 69, 74, 79, 81, 82, 86, 90, 94, 98, 99, 102, 117, 121, 123, 125, 131–134, 138, 140, 141, 145, 149, 151, 154, 156–158, 162, 169, 171, 172, 185, 196
Javadoc, 96

lazy loading, 77
Lisp, 120, 138, 139
loyalty, 152

maintainability, 12, 18, 29, 42, 50, 67, 74, 84, 86, 92, **115**, 115, 164, 172, 178, 182, 187
manipulators, 53
Martin, Robert C., 96
method overloading, 30, 180
metric, 115
mocking, **98**
Mockito, 100
mutability, 74

name, 19
noun, 53, 59
Null Object, 148, 193

object, 19, 23, 43, 50, 165, **186**

222

OpenJDK, 92
optimization, 126

performance, 36, 37, 50, 124
PHP, 31
pointer, 146
polymorphism, 126
procedure, 25, 55
programming
    aspect oriented, 206
    defensive, 149
    functional, 120, 122, **138**
    object-oriented, 18, 46, 61, 72, 76, **113**, 118, 121, 122, 127, 130, 133, 139, 142, 163, 165, 167, 169, 185, 194
    procedural, 55, 65, 113, 119, 146
property
    static, 64
Python, 144

RAII, 216
readability, 61
real world, 58, 152
recoverability, 203
refactoring, 60, 101
reflection, 178
resource, 217

respect, 57, 145, 186
responsibility, 186, 196
Ruby, 20, 24, 167

scope of visibility, 17, 153
setter, 55, 162
side effects, 85
simplicity, 92
Single Responsibility Principle, 28
Singleton Pattern, **133**
state, 42, 44, 151, 153
static method, 46, **117**, 123, 133, 143
sub-routine, 119, 146, 164
synchronization, 89

testability, 115, 172
thread safety, 88
transparency, 39
trust, 185, 200

unit tests, 94, 95, 98
universe, 44, 47
utility class, 47, 118, **132**, 136

variable, 186
    global, 137
verb, 53
virtual method, 209

Made in the USA
Middletown, DE
11 May 2024

54071091R00132